New
Architects

New Architects

A guide to Britain's best young architectural practices

The Architecture Foundation
Supported by the Department for Culture, Media & Sport
Sponsored by British Steel
In association with Glasgow 1999 UK City of Architecture and Design
Edited and produced by Wordsearch Communications

Dedicated to the memory of Sir Peter Hunt
Chairman of Land Securities and Trustee of the Architecture Foundation

Published © 1998 by
Booth-Clibborn Editions
12 Percy Street
London
W1P 9FB

Reprinted 1999

Copyright © 1998 Booth-Clibborn Editions
Copyright © 1998 The Architecture Foundation
Designed by Phillip Evans @ Wordsearch Communications

ISBN 1-86154-018-3

info@internos.co.uk
www.booth-clibborn-editions.co.uk

Printed in Hong Kong

Contents

Introduction by Chris Smith, Secretary of State for Culture, Media and Sport   6

Foreword by Richard Rogers, Chair of The Architecture Foundation   8

How to use this directory by Lee Mallett, Editor   10

The client/architect relationship: 12
Piers Gough
Jim Meldrum
Roland Paoletti
Harry Handelsman
Tony Fretton
Ron German and Peter Rogers
Lesley Chalmers

A-Z of practice profiles   15

Appendix 1: Practice details   133

Appendix 2: Royal Institute of British Architects' Clients Advisory Service   157

Index of practices by region   158

Sponsor's comment   159

Acknowledgements   160

Introduction
Chris Smith
Secretary of State
for Culture, Media
and Sport

Frank Lloyd Wright's observation that "the physician can bury his mistakes, but the architect can only advise his client to plant vines" has an equally sobering corollary: "they should go as far as possible from home to build their first buildings". It has indeed been abroad where many young British architects have confirmed their early promise – Richard Rogers's Pompidou Centre is a case in point – but while we are rightly proud of their success, there has often been less enthusiasm for their innovative designs in this country than overseas. In the year since this book was first published, however, much has been done to promote modern architecture and its culture: I am delighted to introduce this reprint of "New Architects" which, along with the initiatives the Government and others are pursuing, holds out the prospect that inventive modern architecture, and hopefully its practitioners, are coming home.

The major role in ensuring that good architecture flourishes is providing information to those who decide what is built. This book identifies emerging architectural practices of real potential, showcasing exciting work of the highest quality in Ross and Cromarty and Devon, as well as in London and Manchester. It reveals the wealth of talent throughout the country, bringing the best young architects to the attention of both private clients and those with responsibility for the procurement of public buildings: I am extremely pleased that the book has proved so popular that a reprint is called for. Eighteen months on from the original selection, many of those practices featured have already demonstrated that they are headed for greater things.

"New Architects" has helped to make better informed and more confident clients, and given encouragement to those who want to commission better buildings. I am currently engaged in establishing a new lead body for architecture, to operate from the autumn, which I intend should play a similar valuable role: it will actively promote excellence in design, and will seek to prompt reaction from a wider audience of people than has previously considered the buildings around them. Although not exclusively, I will look to the new body to concern itself, like this book, with smaller projects: the high-quality houses, extensions, conversions and shops highlighted here are just as significant as the flagship projects in creating a stimulating and exciting built environment.

But of course excellence in design is crucial to those prestigious projects too. Central Government, as the largest construction client, has not enjoyed a consistent record in commissioning public buildings, but this Government is committed to improving that record, and is determined that design quality should be a key factor in all its procurement processes.

This concern for design is of crucial importance as we enter a period of building such as this country has not experienced since the war. Millions of new homes are required for new lifestyles; demand for hospitals, schools, offices will continue to grow. To meet the challenge of producing environmentally-friendly buildings of which we can be proud, public and private sectors alike must insist on design excellence. We need the gifts of those featured in these pages, and I hope that, along with the initiatives which we in Government are putting in train, this book will help to continue the renaissance of modern architecture in Britain, and will lead to opportunities for these young architects to prove themselves worthy heirs to their world-class predecessors. I look forward to that, and to the next group of emerging British architects featuring in a similar publication.

Foreword Richard Rogers Chair of The Architecture Foundation

Britain is fortunate to enjoy an extensive and culturally diverse generation of professional and talented young architects, but as yet they are relatively unknown. One of the tragedies of our ignorance is that they are so rarely deployed on significant projects: our schools, housing, hospitals, office headquarters, community centres, public squares or parks.

The Architecture Foundation is a charity committed to promoting contemporary architecture and design to the general public and a strong underlying theme running through all of our activities has been to raise the profile of younger architects.

In many countries publicly accessible 'year books' are produced to raise awareness of new practitioners and their work. This first directory for Britain, which will be regularly updated and extended, is significantly the result of a collaboration between the Foundation and the Ministry of Culture, Media & Sport. This is therefore an 'official' exposition of the country's young talent to the myriad of public and private clients whose responsibility it is to commission projects on behalf of us all. Mobilising the enthusiasm, energy and imagination of eager emerging practices on projects that enliven communities, encourage learning and lessen suffering is an important tool in the creation of an inclusive society.

The best architecture relies on enlightened and committed clients, be it in the private sector or in the public arena. It is important to ensure a better understanding of the rich scene in this country, recognised internationally as one of the best in the world. But public appreciation of British architecture tends to focus on a few famous names, so the aim of this project is to widely extend that appreciation.

Apart from providing a practical resource for clients and potential clients, it is also therefore a timely appraisal of the work of Britain's younger practitioners. The directory should not be read as glorification of a few or a finite list — we want to promote quality first and foremost and to give people an understanding of this generation alongside a record of their strengths and professional competency.

In contrast to the UK, continental European countries ensure design is *the* priority in all public building projects. In order to achieve this the selection of architects for all public projects is through a design competition system. Renzo Piano and I were fortunate enough to win the first major French public competition of this type, the Centre Pompidou — we were then in our mid-thirties. Since then the French government has promoted scores of young architects through this process. Through their programme they have succeeded in procuring some of the finest architecture of modern times and in encouraging a whole new generation of architects of which the most notable, Nouvel, Tschumi, Portzamparc and Perrault, are established international figures.

Many of our own historic buildings were designed by young architects and this has been the legacy of great and courageous patrons of the past. As you look through this publication you will notice many projects are small scale or interiors, where are this generation's hospitals and housing projects? The standard of work is extremely high, the opportunity to build extremely limited.

In Britain today we need to do more — clients need to be bold and innovative. Organisations like the Architecture Foundation can lend support and raise awareness of what is possible.

This directory celebrates the diversity of the current generation of emerging practices and should be used as a critical component of a comprehensive selection and competition structure that will mean quality of design in our everyday lives. I wholeheartedly urge clients of small and large projects to integrate the use of this directory in their commissioning process and hope that all readers will find this first edition a useful introduction to the scope of design emerging from Britain today.

From left:
Sir Christopher Wren, aged 29, Kensington Palace 1661-1702.
Robert Adam, aged 32, Kedleston Hall 1760.
CFA Voysey, aged 41, Broadley's Lake Windermere 1898.
Charles Rennie Mackintosh, aged 28, The Mackintosh School of Art 1896-1906.
Philip Webb, aged 28, The Red House 1859.

From left:
Berthold Lubetkin (with Tecton), aged 32, Highpoint 1933-1935.
Alison & Peter Smithson, aged 21 & 24, Huntstanton, Norfolk 1949-1954.
Sir Norman Foster, aged 36, Willis Faber Building 1971-1975.

How to use this book
Lee Mallett
Editor

Choosing an architect is not difficult when you know where to look. This directory, which the Architecture Foundation hopes will be the first of many, is intended as a first stage in the selection process and should function as a practical aid for prospective clients. Apart from brief practice profiles and comments from our assessors alongside images of work, we've also included the telephone numbers and much more detail about each practice's capabilities and experience in the appendix which follows the main section.

Clients should not necessarily expect exactly the same service they might receive from more experienced, established practices. However, as Piers Gough points out in the following selection of comments, young practices usually have to work harder than more established ones, and they tend to do so with enthusiasm and energy and with a fresh eye.

Clients should be aware that there is a very wide range of approaches among the practices featured. While all architects absorb architectural theory as part of their training, some are driven by it more than others. The prospective client should be aware of the need to examine his or her practical requirements carefully in the light of how practices are likely to approach projects and what their capacity and ability appear to be. If you wish to be experimental, be prepared to experiment.

If clients wish to pursue their ideas with more experienced firms then they may like to contact the Royal Institute of British Architects' Clients Advisory Service (see appendix 2 for details). But readers should know that talent within this directory can be applied to large and expensive schemes as much as it can to small projects. Anyone who wants to create any kind of building, or seeks help with the simplest kind of fit out from a chip shop to a new arts centre will find in these pages a firm of architects that can help.

To compile the directory, a two stage process was used. Practices first responded to an open invitation placed in the professional press. The best among these were selected by a panel of five experts. A team of 24 expert assessors then visited each practice to check the information supplied by them and to look at their working practices and conditions. A second panel of experts and lay representatives then reviewed all the reports.

Speaking from my own experience as a client who commissioned a burgeoning practice to work on my home, I definitely got more than I bargained for in the best possible sense and the budget was met almost exactly. But the thing about making architecture, actually building it, is that it remains a craft-based activity and unexpected issues arise which can take time, patience and money to resolve. So while satisfaction can never be guaranteed absolutely, and caution should be exercised, we are pretty certain that there is an immense amount of utility and delight to be found in commissioning new and exciting architects, not least because it can be a journey of discovery for the client that lasts a lifetime.

Not only that but to explore, as the Architecture Foundation has, a new generation of architects and discover so much talent, so much good architecture and so many different and interesting people and ideas has been a real privilege for all those involved. More importantly, there need never be another boring building if the work in this directory is anything to go by.

Lee Mallett is the Deputy Managing Director of Wordsearch Communications, joint editor of Planning in London and former editor of Building Design.

Assessors

Nigel Woolner
Michael Manser
Clyde Malby
Geoffrey Murray
Terry Trickett
Lee Mallett
David Rosen
Jack Pringle
Sutherland Lyall
Robert Bevan
Santa Raymond
Peter Murray
Professor Peter Fawcett
Proessor Roger Stonehouse
Professor Robin Webster
Kester Rattenbury
Adrian Gale
John Kirwan
Professor Charles McKean
Colen Lumley
Deyan Sudjic
John Wells-Thorpe
Marco Piplica
Ann Santry

The client/architect relationship

Piers Gough
Architect

With a young practice, the client is likely to get an increased amount of attention because young practitioners are often the partners themselves. They tend to come fresh to problems, without the baggage that an older practice might bring – and they will be studying fresh research, rather than relying on existing knowledge. Young people often have more energy which they are prepared to use to prove themselves, to stay in business, and since their workload is generally lighter, they usually try harder to make sure schemes work.

Patently there are the advantages of experience but the lack of experience can be overcome with effort and time.

Commissioning a building could be one of the most enjoyable events in one's life, and if one takes that approach, doing it with a young practice is liable to be more elevating than with someone who has done it all before.

One of the basic worries about working with architects is that you'll get what they want, not what you want. If you are a first time or inexperienced client then an older practice is more likely to give you what they want. A young practice should be more flexible and you are more likely to get what you want.

If you are engaged with the trials and tribulations of your architect, struggling with the planners and the contractor, you will get more out of it. You can't just stand back. It is much more important to work things up with the architects. In our experience, the brief – the real brief – only comes out after the first draft designs, and that transforms the brief and it is that process – getting close to the architect – that is important.

Jim Meldrum
Molendinar Housing Association, Glasgow

Having got to know some of the construction professionals involved with refurbishment work on Victorian tenements in the area, we [Reidvale Housing Association] decided on new building projects to look at more radical ways of procuring skills. We decided to go for a limited competition and invited six architects to produce ideas for our Duke Street development. We got some radical ideas. Elder & Cannon who won the competition produced an award-winning traditional four-storey building with generous living spaces. By reducing the common areas and by sinking the floor levels in the living rooms their design created an overall feeling of space and light. The space standards achieved were much greater than one would see in a typical private sector housing development.

We've always worked very closely with the architect throughout the design process and in this way the building was not just a product of the architect's vision but also a tangible product of the committee's own ideas and one of which the community could be proud. Both the architect and ourselves benefited from the cross-fertilisation of ideas. I believe 'lay' people should not only take part in the selection of architects they should become involved in the design process itself in order that they can feel a real sense of ownership.

In the early days of Glasgow's renaissance, committee members were asked why they had got involved and one popular answer was 'to get a bath inside the house'. Things have moved on since then and by working closely with the architect the question is no longer about where the bath goes but what will be the impact of the scheme on the community in general and the immediate environment in particular. So, if you can bring the young, visionary and innovative architect together with the energy, committment and common sense ideas of a lay committee, you will be on to a winner every time. If this directory encourages others to use architects, to get involved and benefit in the way we have in Reidvale then it has got to be a good thing.

Roland Paoletti
Director: Jubilee Line Extension

If you go to a small practice the great benefit is that the owner of the firm is doing the work and not an employee. It's a very different thing and usually means that this is the partners' main chance and they will work day and night to make it happen. A big firm won't do that in quite the same way.

One of the problems that smaller firms face in working on larger public projects is that the client bodies may be filled with bureaucrats who require all kinds of paperwork to be produced. Clients need to realise the real benefits they can get from working with smaller firms and not to require too much bureaucracy, which can smother what the practice has to offer.

Small can be much more effective. There is nothing wrong with a small office. Look at Chris Wilkinson Architect's new Stratford train depot [in east London]. The Financial Times said it was the best building it had ever received for its prestigous Architecture at Work Awards.

The thing about small good practices is that they can attract the brightest and best people to work for them. When firms become big and famous they attract a slightly different kind of talent, or let's say many more people want to work for a famous firm, not all of whom are as talented as they think, or their motives are different. The good small practices just starting out attract people for intellectual and artistic reasons alone.

The architects in this directory are going to produce work that is fresh and close to architectural culture and they are absolutely contemporary. A lot of practices begin very well but then the partners become business people and employ younger people to do their design work for them, not allowing them the freedom they should. So it is sometimes hard with larger firms to get very good design and there can be a terrible uniformity about their work. On the other hand one has to be careful with younger

architects because they can be too fashionable and therefore ephemeral.

As far as choosing an architect goes, my advice would be to personalise things as soon as possible. Get to know the person who is going to be looking after you and take all the time you need to make your enquiries personally. If you get the right person, you won't need all the documentation that can go with the building process. If you pick the wrong person all the documentation in the world won't help you get the job right once it has gone wrong.

Harry Handelsman
Chairman, The Manhattan Loft Company

There is a clear need for a directory like this. When people want to improve their home or their office, or open up a restaurant or shop – whatever it is – they ask 'who do I go to, how can I make it?'. It is not easy to find architects. We should be employing good architects to design all our day-to-day buildings, not just on Lottery-funded projects or major schemes. People should realise that good architects can work on things that have really small budgets just as well as they can on larger projects.

Part of the problem is that architecture and architects are viewed by the public as elitist and people don't understand the kind of friendships that can develop. Developing a working relationship can give a great sense of involvement and satisfaction. The beauty of architecture is that it encourages people to work at it. It is not like buying a car where you just get to choose the colours. If people can engage with new architectural ideas and win some satisfaction from them then they will start to recognise that architecture is very much part of all our lifestyles.

Everybody knows that if you want to buy a suit you have a huge choice of stores to go to, but if you want an architect where do you go? This book represents an opportunity for everybody to realise the role architects and architecture can play in their lives – on everything from a £5000 job to a £100 million job.

Tony Fretton
Architect

Architects often bring inspiration which is far in excess of the brief – the architecture which is imagined is often much more than the client actually has in mind. Any architect who is worth his or her salt does this. But it often takes a long time to find clients as enthusiastic as we the architects are. Clients often want something extremely pragmatic. The important point of change comes when there is a coincidence between the client and the architect's desires.

It is also hard, especially in Britain, for architects to find a place in people's imagination. All of us are in a moment in time when it is very hard not to be nostalgic or conservative. Architecture is very deeply

embedded in society, far more than any of the other arts – and that is an amazing situation.

Architecture is like language, if you depart from accepted usages your readership diminishes drastically. Radicals pay a huge price for pursuing what interests them. When architects set up in practice they accept they have to deal with a set of consensual values.

Architects have to deal with much more complicated states of affairs than other art forms and they start to succeed when they understand the client. You first have to present something that the client understands, and then you can experiment.

All creative work seeks to re-establish cultural values – its not enough simply to service the tastes of the client. We should continue to make work that is questioning, but which also has broad appeal.

The client should feel in some way ennobled by the process. I think that the architecture should amplify the client's life situation. The excitement is not just in the forms, but the way the client's life gets altered and improved. Architects should always ask 'Is it beautiful, Is it practical?'

Ron German and Peter Rogers
Directors of Stanhope Consult, technical advisers to arts organisations and National Lottery Boards

Ron German: Where we have had concerns about smaller practices running substantial Lottery projects, we have tried to marry them up with the right professional team so that they get good back up.

Peter Rogers: Philosophically Britain is very very odd. In many countries it is the custom for smaller more creative practices to hand over the number crunching work to 'bureau d'etude' [larger architectural practices that handle the donkey work]. That has not been the practice in the UK and there is still a resistance to it. The lack of it means there is one less route for helping smaller practices to win Lottery projects and unfortunately some of the larger practices are not very creative.

RG: In this country we tend to make forced marriages between smaller and larger firms and also our contractors haven't developed design skills, unlike the Japanese contractors, and so cannot step into this role of supporting the smaller creative practices. There is a certain arrogance among architects which says 'I don't need to join up with another firm', but there are some opportunities to create very good relationships, rather than the forced ones which have had to be insisted on in some cases.

PR: It is a very difficult leap from the small domestic scale that is the bread and butter of most small practices to the detailed design and project management of larger projects – and God is very much in the details, because if these are not designed properly then all sorts of problems arise.

One of the big problems is the credibility gap between the small first time practice – no matter how good their idea – and the kind of National Lottery-funded client that is probably only going to do this kind of thing once. Often in this kind of situation the client will play far too safe and judge everything on costs alone. So much so that even the consultants may have been picked on this basis and there is no one on the team to fight for the design, so the smaller firms get filtered out at the assessment stage in favour of less creative, bigger firms.

RG: There are now lots of smaller Lottery projects around so the opportunity is there for clients to be more adventurous. Unfortunately many of the Lottery schemes that we have examined are distinctly unadventurous.

PR: We are not really getting excitement or full value for the Lottery's money, so this book is a good idea, but clients must check carefully that these firms can deliver the technical capabilities.

Finally, I would also say that the way in which the Lottery cash is being administered is becoming so hidebound by bureacracy that it is cutting out the more creative architecture.

Lesley Chalmers
Former chief executive of Hulme Regeneration and Kings Cross Partnership

Working on regeneration projects has to be a team effort and client bodies need to find architects who can work well with a team. Architects often have temporarily intense relationships with clients and buildings and then move on to the next one. In Hulme and Kings Cross, what we were trying to do was to put the architects' skills into a pool of expertise and to make schemes that lasts a lifetime.

My experience of architects has not always been good. There is still a lot of arrogance in the profession. Some architects question whether non-designers are qualified to comment on their designs. But the client cannot let them steamroller through their ideas. The best ideas in the world will not be accepted unless the person presenting them is accepted. This sometimes cost us blood, sweat and tears in Hulme.

Multi-disciplinary teams of users and architects are needed on larger schemes but I don't believe that the compromise this may entail has to mean mediocrity. In my five years at Hulme I also had some excellent experiences working with architects. If you go round Hulme now, you can see in the design of the buildings how the issues developed and were dealt with. The client was a thinking client and wasn't frightened of making mistakes, or to move away from what was a winning formula to try new ideas.

In hiring an architect you are not just looking for a product; you are looking for a process and that's where these personal skills are needed.

New
Architects

Adjaye and Russell
Architecture & Design
London

David Adjaye and William Russell formed the practice in 1994 when the two former Royal College of Art classmates collaborated on a series of sets for the televised concert 'Live at the Lighthouse', commissioned by the AIDS charity, London Lighthouse. Before this they had both worked at various well-known practices in Europe and the Far East. Adjaye at David Chipperfield Architects and Chassay Architects, Russell at Tibbalds Colbourne and RMJM Hong Kong. Projects include a private house in Ghana, a house in Dorset for which planning consent has been received and the first of a chain of cafes – Schlotzsky's – which recently opened. The practice has a clutch of residential schemes on the drawing board.

Assessor's comment

Adjaye and Russell are in their formative years as a practice, and the energy and enthusiasm displayed by the partners and their young talented staff is infectious. This practice excels at design, but that is just one element of the complicated process of architecture. Their attention to detail is to be applauded. They are expending all the energy and effort required in the early years of practice and very soon a 'courageous' client will seek out their services and be well rewarded.

Above: Soba Noodle Bar, Soho, London. Left: Schlotzsky's, Oxford Street, London. Far left: office refurbishment, Gorgeous Films, Soho, London.

Alastair Howe Architect
Hertfordshire

Alastair Howe is a sole practitioner and established his practice in 1994. He is currently working on seven different, mainly residential projects including a new-build house in Surrey, to be featured in Build It Magazine, and six new flats in Tulse Hill. Budgets for his completed work have ranged up to £130,000.

Assessor's comment

Alastair Howe seeks to find solutions to clients' problems by designing modern structures. Attention is paid to interior design – including furniture design – and ensuring something special can be created at any budget.

This well-organised office is in an interesting, modern house designed by Howe, which acts as a showcase for his spatial awareness and use of light and materials, creating a memorable home completed to a tight budget. These are strengths that will assist the practice in the future in designing other building types.

Far right: detail of shop conversion to house, Islington, London. All other images: new house, Radlett, Hertfordshire.

AEM
London

Glyn Emrys and Pascal Madoc-Jones met in 1988 whilst working at Rick Mather Architects. The two officially became AEM in 1993 and have established a reputation for transparency, lightness and economy of means in their architecture. The practice's design approach is fundamentally informed by a sense of restraint and control, overlaid by a palette of materials, form and colour.

Assessor's comment

A four-year-old practice that has demonstrated plenty of flair and commitment, including a spectacular planning appeal win for a thoroughly contemporary conversion and extension scheme to an existing Cotswold house and barn – no mean feat – and a fun Japanese restaurant fit-out in Soho. Maximum use of minimum space using colour, drama, sculpted forms and maximised sight lines. Lottery-winning scheme in Norwich for a music-based outreach organisation. Exciting and a safe pair of hands.

Main picture opposite: phase one of Caterpillar Boots' offices and shop, London. Top left: Goldsbrough apartment, kitchen detail and, top right, living space, London. Far right: Caterpillar Boots interior. Right: private apartment, Notting Hill, London.

Allan Murray Architects
Edinburgh

The practice was established in 1992 by Allan Murray and Alexander Fairweather. Murray trained at Harvard and practised in both the UK and USA, with special expertise in urban design. The design aim of the practice includes integration of parallel skills in urban design and landscape architecture. The work often refers to science, literature and art as media for discussing ideas in architecture.

Assessor's comment

Brisk and keen practice expanding on competition and award successes. Highly design-led with lots of models exploring different approaches to each project and its development. Their departure is the analysis of site opportunity and orientation, taking a long view of site potential and client aspirations, with the goal of achieving enquiry, curiosity and excitement in the design within and without. The practice extracts the unforeseen opportunities within the brief – symbolism of the project, imagery and sense of place – and combines them with a transparency of structure, exploitation of views and use of appropriate technology. The resulting characteristic architecture has confident, strongly-modelled forms and striking profile.

Main picture: Peterhead Maritime Heritage Centre (photo: Gavin Fraser).
Left: Scottish National Science Centre, interior view of Great Hall of Science (computer image: 3Di).
Bottom left: Scottish National Science Centre, night view across the Clyde (3Di). Below: MacRobert Arts Centre, Stirling, competition-winning design, night time view.

Anderson Christie Architects
Glasgow

Anderson Christie Architects were established in February 1991 and the practice's core experience is in housing and urban regeneration. Its clients include the Big Issue magazine, housing associations, co-operatives and other community-based groups, the Church of Scotland and the Princess Louise Scottish Hospital at Erskine. The practice is concerned with typology and contextualism in architecture and in exploring the interface between architecture and all of the visual arts. Its workspace on Great Western Road in Glasgow doubles as a gallery.

Assessor's comment

A practice established as a result of the privatisation of architectural services in the provision of social housing in the west of Scotland. Lead by an energetic and highly committed team, including one of the all-too-few senior women partners in a Glasgow architectural practice. Recently completed the imaginative transformation of an old bakery into their own offices, and looking to move beyond housing into other areas of design. Particularly interested in working with the arts and crafts.

Main picture, right and far right: the practice's offices at Great Western Road, Glasgow (photos: Kevin McCourt). Left: Milton Lodge, Dunoon, a home for five adults with learning difficulties.

Allford Hall Monaghan Morris Architects
London

Allford Hall Monaghan Morris was formed in London in 1989, after five years of collaboration between the partners in both practice and education. The partners teach at the Bartlett School of Architecture and have lectured extensively both in the UK and abroad. They have also worked as a team for Britain's largest practice BDP early in their career. Their work includes education, health, transport, leisure and housing projects. Current large scale projects in the office include competition-winning schemes for a bus station, a theatre, an art gallery and a primary school — the latter a prototype for sustainable development. The office is also building a theatre in Hampshire, an apartment block for the Peabody Trust in London, a large private house in Hampstead, a health club and three offices in London's West End.

Assessor's comment

This practice has quickly established a solid reputation via a series of widely-published competition wins and the completion of intelligent and stylish buildings in a wide range of building types. They are a hands-on competent practice who believe in an architecture which is informed by the contemporary scene but whose primary purpose is to create comfortable, exciting environments for its users — an architecture which describes without dictating. Ready for bigger commissions.

Main picture opposite: Canonbury house, London, view from vaults (photo Geoff Beeckman). Top and left: Pool House, Wiltshire (photo Dennis Gilbert). Right: details from St Mary's JMI School, London (photo Dennis Gilbert).

Apicella Associates
London

Apicella Associates is an award-winning practice established by Lorenzo Apicella in 1988. Over the last nine years their work has ranged from the masterplanning proposals for Friedrichstrasse in Berlin to the design of lightweight structures, portable architecture and interiors, such as the second-floor restaurant at Oxo Tower Wharf. Most of the practice's work has been won in invited competitions, and it has been regularly shortlisted or commended in international open competitions.

Assessor's comment

This practice has consistently produced work of the highest standard. Innovative use of materials and ways of building are firmly grounded in an appreciation of the roots of contemporary architecture. A special interest in lightweight structures, membranes and mobile architecture comes from an expertise not only in architecture, but in interior and exhibition design. Establishing a brief is treated as an ongoing process, with feasibility studies and outline proposals being used to test client needs. The practice uses a pro-active approach to monitor the in-use life of their projects. With a clear single vision, design and management becomes a homogeneous process.

Main picture opposite: training, exhibition and conference hall for the design company Imagination (model). Above right: restaurant at Oxo Tower, London. Left: retail outlet for La Perla Lingerie, London. Below: Pavilion, Hong Kong, mobile training structure.

Bareham Andrews Architects
Leeds

Bareham Andrews Architects is a relatively young practice, established in 1993, although Gerard Bareham and Keith Andrews' professional relationship has existed for the past fifteen years. They have experience of a diverse spectrum of building types both within the UK and abroad. Currently working on a project to create a 'modernist' intervention within the shell of two 17th-century town houses in the south of France, and an Education Centre for the Kirkstall Valley Nature Reserve in West Yorkshire. Their work has been exhibited at the Royal Institute of British Architects and the Royal Academy Summer Exhibition and they were included in the Architects Journal's AJ100 Architects Tomorrow and Building Design's Towards 2000 project reviews.

Assessor's comment

Bareham Andrews are a small practice with good ideas and lots of enthusiasm. Their design within tight budgets is well-considered. A small residential extension scheme recently on the drawing board showed some style despite the modest budget.

Main picture and left: proposed Northern Architecture Centre, Newcastle-upon-Tyne. Bottom left: proposed factory, Teeside. Below and below right: model and drawing of proposed Millennium pavilion.

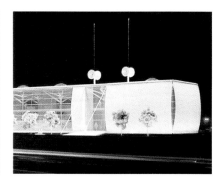

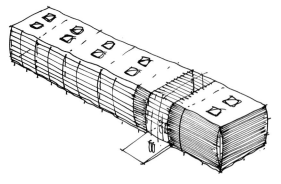

Beevor Mull Architects
Wennington, Cambridgeshire

Beevor Mull Architects were based in London in the 1980s but since 1990 its partners Catrina Beevor and Robert Mull have been based in Cambridgeshire. Both partners hold part-time teaching posts, Mull at the Architectural Association and Beevor at the University of North London. Schemes have included work for housing associations, the local hospital, a day care centre with flats above for elderly people, various residential schemes – including their own house – and experiments with art/architecture collaborations.

Assessor's comment

An architectural studio that is building a reputation out of a combination of architectural practice located in social and community issues and innovatory academic investigations, linking study with teaching. It has a growing variety of building types amongst its built work and projects, and a steady increase in scale of work. While residential work of all kinds is the mainstay of the practice, the grounding in thoughtful and imaginative attitudes to design is leading to a developing body of work in other fields, including urban consultancy. The practice has senior consultancy and design resources. Its fields of influence and operation extends into Europe. Modern in outlook, its own studio and work demonstrate sensitivity to traditional contexts. There are not many modernist architects practising from self-designed new buildings roofed in thatch. Should improve with experience.

Main picture: Cambridgeshire house (photo: James Murphy). Left: Quadrattura – a collaborative artwork with artist Edward Allington – was installed in St Peter's Church, Cambridge, accompanied by an exhibition. Right: pub interior, London (photo: Ian Kalinowski).

Bere : Architects
London

Bere Architects was founded in 1994 by its principal architect, Justin Bere, after parting from Eco-ID Ltd which he co-founded with colleagues from Michael Hopkins & Partners. Initially working on bespoke furniture design and manufacture, and small-scale structural glass additions to listed buildings, Bere Associates quickly developed a reputation for rigorous detailing and innovative use of materials and components. Projects include one-off houses and new-build residential developments, a rural art gallery, urban planning and several large-scale commercial and retail projects.

Assessor's comment

This small practice is strongly led by Justin Bere who takes a craftsman-like intensive approach to all office projects. Attention to the smallest detail is impressive and this is strongly shown in furniture and lighting design. Management is professional and responsible using a management handbook, which draws heavily on RIBA established procedures. Meticulous care is taken over all project work, which currently ranges from product design to buildings up to £1 million in value.

Right: Pizza Express restaurant, City of London (photo: Peter Cook). Left: Falklands War Memorial proposal, Falkland Islands. Below: Ripley House conservatory, London (photo: Michael Heyward). Bottom left: conservatory structural support detail.

Birds Portchmouth Russum
London

The practice was established in 1989, the three partners having previously worked for the office of James Stirling, Michael Wilford & Associates as project leaders on various prestigious projects in Britain and overseas. The practice is renowned within the profession for the stunning architectural ideas and imagery it has produced in a series of competition entries for public projects, including the Museum of Scotland, Morecambe sea front and the design initiative organised by The Architecture Foundation called Croydon – The Future. Current work includes a £95 million masterplan for Laganside Development Corporation in Belfast and providing architectural and artistic services to transform a section of the A13 in London for the Department of Transport, a £12 million project. They are also masterplanning a new civic space in the heart of Leicester.

Assessor's comment

The three partners (supplemented by an offshore partner based in New York) made a name for themselves soon after collaborating and winning an open competition to design a new multi-storey car park in Chichester. The design was built and attracted critical acclaim and won five architectural awards. Few emerging practices have success so soon but the partners are a trio of huge creativity and competence. As yet their other completed work is limited and small scale but it shows the same dedication and skill and will certainly lead them to continued success.

Left and top far left: the competition and award-winning Chichester car park in West Sussex. Top near left: house refurbishment, Haberdasher Street, London. Right: the Croydon Culture Drome, night view produced for The Architecture Foundation initiative, Croydon – The Future.

Boyarsky Murphy Architects
London

Nicholas Boyarsky and Nicola Murphy graduated from the Architectural Association in 1988 and 1989 and worked for a number of well-known practices, including Zaha Hadid and Michael Hopkins, before establishing their own practice in 1993. They have built a number of domestic projects and interiors, as well as shops, offices and other retail outlets in London.

Assessor's comment

Experimental atelier with reasonable experience of residential, retail and restaurant projects and currently co-designers of the new Law Courts in Nicosia in Cyprus. Especially interested in exploring the possibilities of glazing and cast materials, and conceptual experimentation. Not for the faint-hearted, totally pragmatic or uncommitted patron. They have worked on a number of housing schemes, buildings and urban studies in Europe and were prize-winners in the Europan housing competition for The Hague, Netherlands in 1996 – a testing arena.

Main picture, left and right: Belsize house interior, exterior and balcony detail, London (photos: Helene Binet). Far left: tombstone detail, London.

Brady & Mallalieu
London

The practice was formed in 1987 by Angela Brady and Robin Mallalieu, both of whom have a wide experience of many building types. Projects in the office range up to a £3.5 million budget and the practice is working on several Lottery bids, mainly in London. A private housing scheme of 24 flats and 12 houses is under way in north London together with a Foyer scheme in Limerick, Ireland, a housing and training scheme for homeless young people. Other recent schemes include a community centre for an Asian action group, a women's football centre, various offices and residential schemes. The practice believe that an ordered and consistent approach to design, combining creativity and management skills, are the foundations of a good building project.

Assessor's comment

Attention to detail together with a prodigious output are a hard combination for a small practice to achieve, but Brady & Mallalieu manage it repeatedly. A professional and forward-looking CAD-equipped office, they are experienced in both new-build and sensitive but contemporary additions to historic buildings across a broad range of building types. An easily identifiable 'house style' is avoided in favour of strongly site-responsive solutions.

Although the partners are informed by tradition, this is reworked as an evolutionary abstraction, avoiding the historicist or the pastiche. Quality of materials and a skilful handling of colour are always evident in their work. It has won them awards in the UK and Ireland. The practice size means that the partners can be closely involved in all jobs.

Left: rear view of of the School of Architecture and Interior Design for the University of North London, Holloway Road. Right: view of main facade, Holloway Road (photos: Dennis Gilbert). Below: Reception area of office interior, The Irish Tourist Board, London (photo: Andrew Lang Photography).

Brookes Stacey Randall
London

The practice has extensive experience in a wide variety of building types, from the total reconstruction of a major railway station to a boathouse on the River Thames. Their in-house R&D has enabled them to design innovative architectural projects, including collaboration on the Thames Water Tower which demonstrates the use of energy-saving systems.

Assessor's comment

A strong interest in technology runs throughout the practice, although it would be hard to classify them into one architectural camp. Its design for West Croydon Station could be described as high tech while the glass boathouse which cantilevers elegantly over the Thames is positively Miesian. Technology is handled elegantly and with a human touch. A committed and highly competent practice, it has experience of a wide variety of work – pop stars' lofts, railway stations, bridges and refurbishment work. The practice also collaborated on the design of one of the few pure landmark buildings of recent years – the Thames Water Tower at Shepherd's Bush roundabout, west London.

Main picture opposite and right: The Boating Pavilion, Streetley-on-Thames, Berkshire (photo: Peter Durant). Left: Thames Water Tower, Shepherds Bush roundabout, west London (photo: Peter Durant). Above: Enschede Integrated Interchange, Holland (photo: Willem Franken).

Bryant and Priest Architecture
Warley, Birmingham

A Midlands-based practice, founded in 1976 which has a very broad range of experience in most sectors and is currently working on the design development and site operations for The Drum, a national Black/Asian cultural arts centre in Birmingham – a £2.5million Arts Lottery-funded conversion of an existing building. Other projects underway include conversions and new additions to an existing tower block and podium at Newhall Street, Birmingham to provide 76 new apartments, restaurant, offices and car parking and an indoor cricket centre jointly with David Morley Architects for Warwickshire County Cricket Club.

Assessor's comment

Bryant and Priest have an impressive self-assurance, based on several years of success while working in other firms. Both partners have gained design awards – Civic Trust, Housing and others. Their accomplishments demonstrate a breadth of experience unusual in so fresh a practice. The office looks pretty efficient with short lines of communication. The technical and administrative back-up is strong, including family links, where a previous Bryant practice was in business in the area for the last 20 years.

The practice is informal and ambitious. It is well resourced and clearly unafraid to reach beyond its immediate grasp. There is considerable potential on offer here.

Above and below, far right: Components House loft apartment interior, Birmingham. Left: 19 Newhall Street, Birmingham, interior shot of inserted mezzanine and stairs and below right, model of the The Drum, National Black/Asian Cultural Arts Centre, Birmingham.

Carter Reynolds
London

Tom Reynolds and Howard Carter, who formed the practice in 1995, have a combined experience of 25 years working at highly-respected practices, such as the Renzo Piano Building Workshop, Genoa, Sir Norman Foster & Partners and the Richard Rogers Partnership. The initiative was taken to set up a new operation providing the same innovative, high quality secure service to a wider range of projects. The practice has tackled residential, commercial, transport, health and education projects in the last two years.

Assessor's comment

The two partners in this small practice have an impressive pedigree, working for leading practices on large, high-profile schemes before setting up a studio together. At present their work as a practice has been comparatively small-scale, but this has allowed significant partner involvement in every project and a confidence in managing projects. This safe pair of hands, they hope, inspires clients to reach out for more innovative solutions, 'wringing every drop of poetry out of the dry bones of functionalism'. The streamlined office appears well organised and professional, working almost entirely on CAD-based workstations. The practice produces a highly-polished modernism, tending towards the minimalist but using rich materials, elegantly detailed rather than puritan white on white. At present, residential and small-scale medical work makes up the bulk of their portfolio.

Above and left: Cavendish Road Surgery, London and below right, three computer images of Great Cornard Upper School, Sudbury, Suffolk.

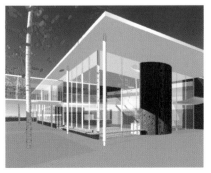

The practice was established in November 1994, and commissions have been for residential, workplace, health, education and exhibition design projects. The work addresses the balance of heterogeneity and homogeneity in architecture, and the idea of configuring a spatially and programmatically sustainable architecture; one where the phenomenological and universal transcend the purely functional.

Assessor's comment

Buschow Henley are a cerebral firm whose projects are carefully considered. Their primary interest lies in how the architect may respond to the individual, creating humane and eventful architecture. Inspiration is drawn from contemporary art and city life and this extends also to creating individual pieces of furniture for specific clients.

Main picture, left: 'Padded Cell' for advertising agency HHCL, Kent House, London. Above and below: Prospect House offices, London. Right top: offices for Michaelides & Bednash, London. Below right: model of warehouse conversion scheme for apartments, London.

Caruso St John
London

Caruso St John Architects' projects range in
scale from private houses to public buildings
and the practice has won prizes in several
international competitions for public buildings
and urban scale developments. Their ideas and
their work have generated substantial interest
and coverage in the architectural press and
elsewhere. In 1995 the practice won an
international competition to design the new
4500 sq m Walsall Art Gallery which is now
under construction. Other work includes a
surgery in Surrey, a new pub in Walsall, a
warehouse refurbishment in Clerkenwell in
London and exhibition designs. Partners Adam
Caruso and Peter St John have been visiting
critics at the Georgia Institute of Technology
in Atlanta, KTH Stockholm, University College
Dublin, Academy van Bouwkunst in
Amsterdam, the Technical University of Nova
Scotia and the School of Architecture at
Cambridge University.

Assessor's comment

Caruso St John is an atypical practice in the
sense that it combines the activities of
teaching, research and successful practice –
the latter quite deliberately based on entering
architectural competitions. Their £15.7million
winning design for Walsall art gallery and a
public square funded by Lottery money is due
for completion in 1998. The partners say that
their work is interested in authenticity in
building and in contemporary urban structure,
a contextualism which engages the everyday
and a spatial quality which tries to encourage
a social transparency.

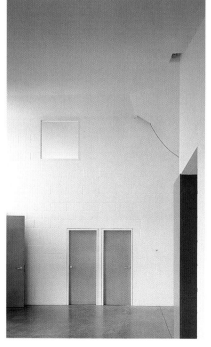

Main picture opposite and
right: studio house, London,
exterior and interiors.
(photos: Helene Binet)
Above and left: private
house, Lincolnshire (photo
Helene Binet) Far left: model
of Walsall Art Gallery, now
under construction.

Cottrell and Vermeulen Architecture
London

The partnership was set up in 1992. Prior to this both partners worked on the restoration of the Unite d'Habitation by Le Corbusier in Marseilles. Their work covers a variety of building types, both public and private, tackling issues from the regeneration of the city to working within the natural landscape. Most recent projects have been for schools, community groups and churches, providing a contemporary expression for the activities involved, in conjunction with the needs of both user and surrounding community.

Assessor's comment

A practice with a wide range of work and a particular interest in community projects, churches, housing, the arts, sports, leisure and even set design for video production. It brings to this diverse range of projects a gentle sensitivity for bold solutions and a deft use of colour to enhance low cost schemes. The partners believe in the benefits of collaboration for the best results; not just with its clients but with every other participant in a project. This is an interesting and capable partnership.

Main picture opposite: Westborough Primary School lunch boxes, Westcliff-on-Sea, Essex (photo: Dennis Gilbert). Top: Westborough Primary School (photo: Dennis Gilbert). Above left: Milton Hall School, Westcliff-on-Sea, Essex (photo Dennis Gilbert). Left and right: Newmartin Centre Communal Hall and St Martin's Church, east London (photo: Paul Ratigan).

David Mikhail Architects
London

David Mikhail became a chartered architect in 1988 and went on to enjoy success in a number of international competitions, most notably a winning scheme for the remodelling of Zagreb. Since the practice was founded in 1992, he has worked on a number of projects, including new build residential, refurbishment and extending properties in conservation areas, retail outlets, an arts workshop and a gallery.

Assessor's comment

David Mikhail designed a beautiful residential mews scheme in London with a great glazed and white-washed brick facade, which won a lot of publicity and demonstrated plenty of ability. He has much urban domestic experience and is beginning to move on to bigger things – like a Lottery bid print workshop and gallery. Good use of colour, materials and space.

Left, below, above and main picture opposite: 41-43 Pottery Lane, west London, a new build house. Below right: 10 Acar Road, London, apartment refurbishment and extension.

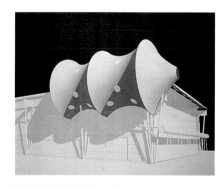

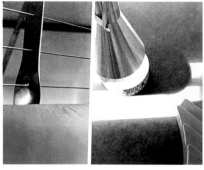

David Sheppard Architect
Plympton St Maurice, Devon

The practice was formed in 1987 to offer a green approach to design and to execute buildings incorporating the latest in modern technology to arrive at appropriate, innovative and stimulating solutions. Use of timber, fabric, rammed earth, horticulture and grass roof construction. Currently designing six earth sheltered buildings that incorporate this technology along with wind, solar and photovoltaic enhancement.

Assessor's comment

This is very much the single practitioner office run from home, a house in the centre of Plympton St Maurice. There is a part-time secretary and two part-time technicians working elsewhere whose services, whether for CAD work or technological support, are called upon as necessary.

The work tends to be extreme wtih many lively but untried ideas. This exuberance is supported by a clientele who appear not to be concerned by being led down uncharted paths.

There is a slightly chancy quality to the technology, but there is no doubt that there is a very talented designer at work.

Below and far right: Matthew Architecture Gallery at the University of Edinburgh (photo: Gavin Fraser). Right: Housing for Horizon Housing Association, South Gyle, Edinburgh (photo: Keith Hunter). Second right: Stevenson house alterations, Morningside, Edinburgh (photo: Gavin Fraser).

E & F McLachlan Architects
Edinburgh

Ewen and Fiona McLachlan both qualified as architects in the early 1980s, and in 1990 their practice was established in Edinburgh. Both partners have been involved in teaching architectural design at the University of Edinburgh, and were instrumental in the founding of the Matthew Architecture Gallery, the principal venue for architectural exhibitions in Scotland. The practice won its first invited competition for new housing in Edinburgh in 1995 with a contract of over £1.1 million for 27 flats completed last year. Two further competition wins followed, a second housing project and a centre for small businesses.

Assessor's comment

A tight, controlled, competition-winning design office sharing a Victorian business chambers overlooking North Bridge. Hands-on design creation and project management by the two partners – from exhibition design to housing schemes. Work thoroughly informed by deep knowledge of contemporary Europe (authors of interactive Database of European architecture) with high computer utilisation. Equal interest in design and practical building founded on prior large-scale experience. Focused on getting the most from very little, creating unforeseen opportunities for clients through changing perceptions of space using plane and colour.

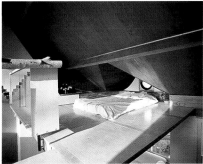

de Rijke Marsh Morgan
London

Alex de Rijke has worked both in London, with practices such as Rick Mather Architects and Tchaik Chassay, and in Amsterdam. The range of disciplines within the practice, including strong interior design skills and ongoing collaborations with artists and technical consultants, has allowed for an informed diversity in design approach to each project. A series of urban design proposals for the improvement of Plymouth city centre has just been completed.

Assessor's comment

This small and committed practice has the feeling of an atelier, perhaps reflecting de Rijke's teaching experience at the Architectural Association and the Royal College of Art – which he has now given up to concentrate on practice and Morgan's teaching at Chelsea College of Art and Design. Each project is driven by a strong concept and by the site rather than one defined style. They describe their approach as economy of means with expressive and inventive use of materials. The result is fresh and contemporary architecture which is exciting and interesting. The mainstay of its recent workload has been the design of a chain of American fitness centres which reflects the practice's ability to solve problems in unconventional ways as well as their ability to stick to the hard-nosed aspects of budget and schedule.

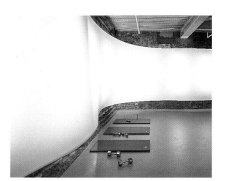

Main picture opposite, above, left and right: house conversion, Cornwall.
Left: gymnasium, America Square, City of London (photo: Michael Mack).
Right: gymnasium, shower/changing area, Berkeley Square, Mayfair, London (photo: Michael Mack).

East
London

East is a young critical practice which combines architectural, landscape, planning and urban design projects with research and teaching. Much of the practice's work has concentrated on a specific area of East London and the Lower Thames, often linked directly to broader regeneration strategies, developing a close knowledge and involvement with the processes of urban change.

Assessor's comment

East has been building their reputation on thoughtful urban design and regenerative work, often for community groups or local authorities, eschewing the fashionable shops and lofts fodder that many young practices cut their teeth on. Consequently, while they have built little, they have an interesting portfolio and a professional approach to dealing with the demands of public clients. This work has included successful Lottery submissions and detailed appraisals and strategies for the revitalisation of run-down or redundant areas of cities. Planning and landscaping skills come to the fore here. Their completed architectural work is in the functional tradition and avoids the bespoke in favour of easily available materials used innovatively; an example of which is stove-baked, brightly painted paviors suggested in one project. Art installations and bold typographics also characterise their work which they describe as 'anti-formist'. East have worked extensively with other practices and appear instinctively collaborative.

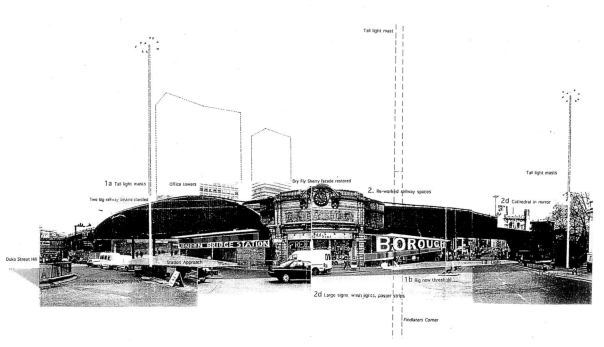

Above and right: East were one of six practices, selected from more than 100, to consider how parts of the streets and public spaces in Southwark, south London, could be improved, under the Future Southwark Initiative, organised by The Architecture Foundation. East is implementing a £1 million package of improvements. Top left: Stratford Advice Arcade, London. Below: Brader Perryman, advertising agency, London.

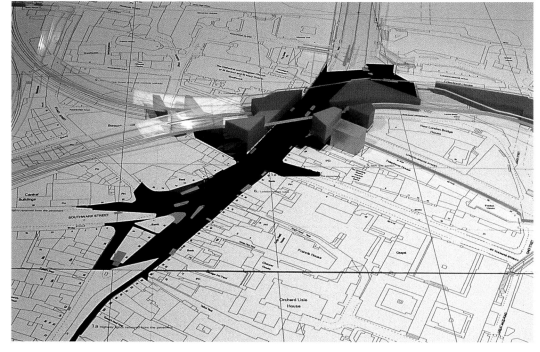

FAT
London

FAT (the acronym stands for Fashion: Architecture:Taste) is a multi-disciplinary architecture and design practice with five principals; four architects and one artist. They have a reputation for imaginative and often provocative work and have been widely published. Apart from experience in the design of leisure environments, they have also completed a number of residential and office projects in Europe and the UK and several of the principals have strong academic connections.

Assessor's comment

FAT is a creative practice widely admired for its design, architecture and art output. The practice is focused in two main experimental directions. One is looking at how art and media forms can influence architecture and how blurring of their boundaries can produce more interesting work. The second takes the direction of an inclusive approach to design which involves using and reusing conventional objects and materials in unexpected and imaginative ways which are understandable to the lay world as well as to the architectural community.

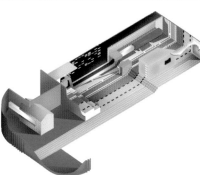

Above: Chez Garson, house conversion, London (photo: Joshua Pullman). Above right: model for Scala Foyer Bar, Kings Cross, London. Left and far left: drawing and built interior for the Brunel Rooms nightclub, Swindon (photo: Andy Keales). Right: house conversion, Brixton, south London.

Main picture opposite: Futureworld House, Milton Keynes. Above, new shop for Giulio, Cambridge. Left: Blospace, an extension to a house in London. Below: Ellis-Miller House, Prickwillow, Cambridgeshire. All photos: Timothy Soar.

Ellis-Miller Architects & Designers
Cambridge

Jonathan Ellis-Miller formed this practice in 1992. It has addressed a broad range of work, including new buildings, interiors and the conversion of historic structures. Notable projects include the partner's own house at Prickwillow, Cambridgeshire, a striking and elegant contemporary house, and an equally powerful statement, Futureworld House at Milton Keynes. The practice also designed an award-winning office building in the City of London.

Assessor's comment

A small, young architectural studio with zealous ambitions to develop into a leading practice. Its approach is project-centred aimed at providing the best solution to the subject in hand, be it energy efficiency, media or communications. While it is determinedly modernist in outlook, it has experience with listed buildings and in providing the special design attention needed. The practice has highly developed promotional abilities and attitudes to design quality. It prides itself on presentation skills — employing state-of-the-art 3D imaging techniques — and on best practice in organising and managing projects. The range of built work, generally, has been small-scale, but this has attracted exceptional notice and awards; projects on site and on the drawing board are getting larger. The built work represents a level of design achievement, forward-looking in its technology, if shorter in originality and conception than the cutting-edge aspirations of the practice.

Above, left and far left:
Computer images of
Yokohama International
Port Terminal, Japan.
Main picture opposite and
below: Bermondsey Square
proposal, London.

Foreign Office Architects Ltd
London

The partners Alejandro Zaero Polo and Farshid Moussavi teach at the Architectural Association and are visiting lecturers at other national and international schools. Their work at the AA includes a research programme on urban projects. Other projects have included a study for the redevelopment of the government centre in Bonn, Germany, a commission for ideas to develop a new island near China, a private house in Sussex, a design for an extension to a home for the elderly also in Sussex and a design for a villa in Madrid. Their work has been written about extensively, more so since they won the grand prize in the Yokohama International Ferry Terminal competition in Japan. This is a £150 million scheme.

Assessor's comment

A very creative but also pragmatic approach to design. With the business experience obtained from their work on the Yokohama ferry terminal, new international competition projects and now potential UK medium-sized projects, the office is well placed to take on work which will be dealt with on a sound professional basis. 'We avoid recipes; we approach every project as if we had not done another before. Learning to find every situation surprising helps us to develop the maximum architectural potential from each commission,' say the partners. Because of their creative skills, they are continually being asked to conferences and seminars around the world to 'give away' their thoughts and ideas. It is time they had the opportunity to put them into practice.

Gollifer Associates
London

The practice bases its work on social and ecological values, creative discussion with the client and the context of the project: by forming an understanding of the way people interact with their environment and exploring their needs, the solution will become more appropriate. This approach may mean that aspects of their architecture depart from the conventional, but it always maintains the central values of a sense of place, integrity of ideas and beauty of execution. The practice has a wide range of experience of small to medium size projects, mainly in central London.

Assessor's comment

A competent and caring practice, very hands on. The practice manual was impressive for such a relatively small practice. They appear to have coped well with their £7.2million project, the National Glass Centre in Sunderland, and should be able to take on another large projects in addition to their more regular £100,000 to £200,000 projects.

Above: Atelier restaurant, Beak Street, London. Left and far left: Ally Capellino fashion store, Sloane Street, London.
Right: model, National Glass Centre, Sunderland (photo: Andrew Putler).

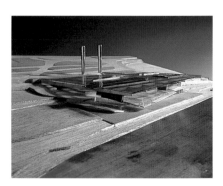

Harper Mackay
London

Prior to setting up their own practice, David Harper worked for Nicholas Grimshaw & Partners and Ken Mackay for Jeremy Dixon & Edward Jones in London. The practice has an eclectic and extensive cross-section of work which has encompassed new buildings, green field architecture, factories, urban infill of city sites, renovation, high fashion shops, restaurants and low-cost housing. Their forte, however, has proved to be the imaginative and contemporary reconfiguration and fit-out of London's burgeoning media company offices in which field they are rapidly becoming market leaders.

Assessor's comment

David Harper and Ken Mackay established Harper Mackay in 1987. As well as architectural design, the practice is known for interior, retail, packaging and furniture design; it also advises clients on branding and advertising issues.

The practice has built a successful reputation working for image and media-aware clients. It employs leading edge IT techniques for communicating through innovative and stimulating graphics. Their work is international with projects from New York to Japan.

The practice is well-established and has increased its management systems to support its expanding workload. Adept marketeers who are quickly moving into the big time.

Above and left: Bertorelli's restaurant and brasserie, Charlotte Street, London. Right: Central Broadcasting re-fit, Birmingham.

Hawkins/Brown Architects
London and Nottingham

Hawkins/Brown was formed in 1988 after the two partners had worked together at Rock Townsend. While developing a reputation for innovative commercial work, they have designed a series of popular community arts and education buildings that have led them to work on university projects. Their work as planning consultants and urban designers led to their appointment as architects to the Henry Moore Foundation at Perry Green.

Assessor's comment

The practice has recently merged with Maber Associates in Nottingham to give a more diverse spread of work. They have a very hands on, busy feel and currently all jobs are directed by either Roger Hawkins or Russell Brown. They have clearly achieved much and have the potential to expand further; what they do at present is many types of refurbishment for a whole range of new uses. Railtrack and London Underground projects should give them good corporate client experience.

Far left and left: University of Southampton (photos; James H Morris). Main picture right and below: South Dock Marina, London Docklands (photo: Peter Durant). Above: Birmingham Institute of Art and Design refectory.

Opposite: Centenary Building, University of Salford. Above: St Catherine's College, Oxford. Below right: Centenary Building, University of Salford and far right: City Road surgery, London.

Hodder Associates
Manchester and London

Hodder Associates is a Manchester and London-based practice with a growing reputation through competition wins and awards. Their work seeks to extend and transform the language of modernism and attain a sense of permanence. Their range of projects include medical centres, universities, galleries, golf clubhouses and swimming pools. The practice won the first ever prestigious Stirling Prize in 1996.

Assessor's comment

The approach of this practice is characterised by the quality and clarity of its architecture and by its insistence on quality of service through a close working relationship with both clients and contractors. The architecture demonstrates a commitment to the developing traditions of modernism and the understanding of context and place. It is considered at all scales with a close attention to detail. The office has established a maturity and cohesion of approach to practice which allows it to produce buildings of innovation and sophistication with assurance and, often, to a limited budget. It is an approach which has led to its record of prestigious national awards and competition wins.

Hudson Featherstone
London

The practice was formed by two partners, Anthony Hudson and Sarah Featherstone, who have been working together for the last five years. They have established a reputation for modern and innovative work which has been publicly recognised in winning the Royal Fine Art Commission & Sunday Times Building of the Year Award for Baggy House in 1995 and a Civic Trust Award in 1996. Together with lecturing at the Royal Institute of British Architects and schools of architecture around the UK, the practice's work has been included in a number of exhibitions including 'How Did They Do That?', an exhibition conceived and curated for the RIBA, which set out to de-mystify the process of designing and making buildings.

Assessor's comment

This practice has a reputation for innovative modern work. So far it has been at a small scale – award-winning houses and nightclubs, for example – but it covers a surprisingly wide spread of building types, from schools to historic building refurbishments. The two principals stress that they don't impose a particular style on their clients, but that their design involves thinking hard about their brief and being prepared to re-think it when standard solutions are likely to produce mediocre results. They are comfortable with the idea of researching innovative technologies if that makes for more economical building. Each project involves close working relationships with clients in the search for wonderful spaces and affordable buildings.

Above: Baggy House, private residence, North Devon (photo: Jo Reid). Main picture opposite, right and far right, the pool garden at Baggy House (photos: Tim Brotherton). Left: Blue Note bar, London (photo: Tim Goffe).

Harrison Ince Architects
Manchester

Established in 1989, Harrison Ince has gained a reputation for projects from bar and restaurant design, housing and sheltered housing to commercial, industrial and leisure developments; small-scale interior design projects to multi-million new build developments. They have emerged as one of the more creative practices in the region with numerous design awards.

Assessor's comment

The practice has a lot of experience in work for the brewing and catering industry, and that still provides its major source of work. Two of its latest buildings, the Barca bar and restaurant and the Mash and Air complex of bars and restaurants, have broken out of the Chef-and-Breweresque mode. Barca is fun, popular and modish; Mash and Air, the conversion of an existing building, is equally popular and is more accomplished.

The practice has a lot of experience, it is enthusiastic, has good client relationships (including an informal procedure of follow up after completion for feedback). They also have a very inventive, researched and tactile approach to the use of materials.

The Communique Offices were completed in 1996, and the G-site hotel and restaurant, which has just received planning approval.

The office is well organised and works as an 'open house' practice with fortnightly design forums in which all the practice is involved and which clients attend.

Above: Barca Bar/Restaurant, Catalan Square, Manchester. Above left: Barca Arches, Catalan Square. Far left and left: offices, Communique, Manchester.

Hugh Broughton Architects
London

Hugh Broughton Architects was established in 1995. Broughton had previously worked for four years as a project director at Troughton McAslan Architects, and for 18 months in Spain, writing articles for British journals as well as books on recent Madrid architecture and minimal architecture in London. The practice has had successful lottery bids for a new building and a feasibility study.

Assessor's comment

A small practice with Hugh Broughton very much the sole practitioner calling on two other architects to help as dictated by workload. Has undertaken a range of small-scale work with close attention to detail, achieving a high architectural quality. The general attitude of the practice is friendly and outgoing; clients would get a high standard of personal service from Hugh Broughton supported by his team.

Above: toilets refurbishment, Congress House, London. Above right: apartment, Holland Park, London (photo: Carlos Dominguez). Right: model shot, District Girl Guides headquarters, Wimbledon, London (photo: Andrew Putler). Far right and left: warehouse apartment, London (photo: Carlos Dominguez).

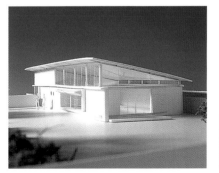

Left and right: Apartment Langham, Mount Bowdon Cheshire. Above: Commercial Wharf, Manchester.
Above right: Atlas Bar, Deansgate, Manchester.

Ian Simpson Architects
Manchester

Ian Simpson and Rachel Haugh established Simpson Associates in 1987 and were joined by new director Charles MacKeith to form Ian Simpson Architects in 1994. Current projects total in excess of £44million and are located across the country, many of them competition winners.

Their new build Foyer, a transitional home for homeless young people, will be completed in Birmingham in April 1998. Their project was the winning scheme in The Architecture Foundation's 1992 competition with Shelter, the campaign for the homeless.

Assessor's comment

Since its formation 12 years ago the practice has established a considerable record of competition wins and a reputation for sensitive and innovative buildings. Besides a wide range of new buildings, the practice has plenty of experience in the restoration and conversion of historic and listed buildings and for preparing successful bids for Lottery funding. It also has extensive experience of urban renewal at all scales, from the city centre to small groups of buildings, and working with community groups and other agencies to produce elegant and thoughtful buildings in response to tight, complex situations. The office works in project teams with regular design sessions and critiques involving all the directors and members of the practice.

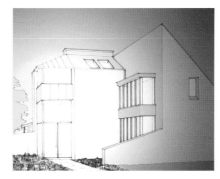

Above left: proposed new farmhouse, Perthshire. Left, above and right: new house at Carrieburn Wood, Perthsire.

John Brennan Architect
Edinburgh

The practice believes there is a new consensus of environmental awareness, having at last moved away from an almost exclusive fixation with energy conservation. Factors such as the re-use of building components and the specification of non-toxic materials play an ever-increasing role. They seek to harness these and integrate them without self-consciously resorting to 'green tokenism'. Within Scotland, the practice has embarked on a number of projects that seek to re-invent rural forms, from modest croft housing to producing a landmark house in the heart of a working farm.

Assessor's comment

Recently established computer-based micro office, overlooking Leith Walk, specialising in contemporary rural design and construction, from an ecological/sustainable perspective. The practice has a particular interest in timber technology, and how construction interacts with the rural economy. Involved in procuring buildings, construction skills and adapting systems. It has one full time partner, supplemented as needed. Brennan seeks to demonstrate how economic rural building, and the sustainable agenda, are compatible with fine modern buildings, farmhouses and steadings.

All pictures opposite and above: John Pardey's house, Lymington, Hampshire (photo: Richard Bryant, Arcaid). Left and right: family house refurbishment, Sway, Hampshire.

Knott Architects
London

The partnership was formed by brothers George and Tom Knott in 1994, founded on extensive accumulated design and practice experience in the UK, Berlin and Ahmedabad in India. They have expertise in working with existing buildings, modelling light and space with sympathetic contemporary interventions.

Assessor's comment

Knott Architects' thoroughly modernist approach is exemplified by their faith in the self-expression of materials. Their work is consequently characterised by precision and robust restraint rather than the precious and genteel, using both the commonplace in new ways and bespoke elements. The complex is made to look simple by honing down to legible essentials.

The partners bring extensive organisation experience with large building projects to bear on their carefully selected schemes. They work closely with clients to develop a brief which raises the clients' own expectations and engagement with architecture. They have little experience of new build – although both partners have this experience as project architects with larger firms.

All pictures: loft conversion, Wardour Street, Soho, London.

Below: Visual Arts Centre, The Gymnasium, Gallery of Modern Art, Edinburgh. Right: National Library of Scotland, support facilities, Sighthill, Edinburgh. Far right: West Shore Business Centre, Granton, Edinburgh. Bottom right: Lee Boyd Partnership design studio.

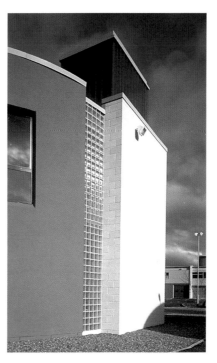

Lee Boyd Partnership
Edinburgh

The practice was founded on a commitment to design excellence, whether buildings, interiors or items of furniture. The office is supported by model-making, graphic and audio-visual, materials research and CAD. The three partners, Stephen Boyd, Scott Lee and Douglas Fraser are actively involved with all projects.

Assessor's comment

A brightly-coloured, busy, briskly-managed, paperless office converted from a police station as a showcase of the practice's own design – particularly in relation to materials, colour and sensuous space. Very contemporary and up front with hands-on design partners. They enjoy creating contemporary opportunities from new-build or refurbishment – from interior institutional refits to entire warehouses, and cheap storage to display cases. Particular effort and time is spent on the selection of materials and detail design; getting in close and creating something special from a necessity.

Loader and Brown Architects
London

Loader and Brown Architects were formed in 1993 with a winning entry to a competition for housing in Gävle, Sweden. Both partners had worked in offices in London since the mid 1980s on projects ranging from office buildings, schools, social housing, private housing and domestic and retail interiors. A concern for the intelligent use of natural and man-made resources is a central principle of their design approach.

Assessor's comment

Winners of a European competition to insert housing into an historically sensitive prison in Gävle in Sweden, and commended for their proposals to create a new living environment on the redundant airbase at Upper Heyford, Oxfordshire. Some urban domestic experience and reconstructive suggestions for inner London housing estates. Exquisite attention to detail, using a sober, but powerful palette. Very sensitive, almost restrained approach that looks long-lasting. Serious, sensitive players.

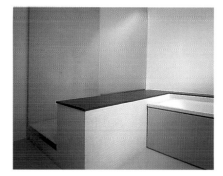

Above and right: apartment, Camden, London. Below: Dartmouth Park Nursery.

Below: Pizza Express, Stockbridge, Edinburgh (photo: Keith Hunter). Far left: Pizza Express, Queensferry Street, Edinburgh (photo: Keith Hunter). Left: model of The Scottish Poetry Library, the Holyrood Project, Edinburgh (photo: Gavin Fraser).

Malcolm Fraser Architects
Edinburgh

The practice believes in a simple, enriched modernism. Because they enjoy working with a client and assisting inception, they have not (as yet) entered competitions; this may change. They have concentrated on doing small jobs well, which has led to larger jobs; the practice has grown from two to 14 people in the last year.

Assessor's comment

Thriving collaborative office in Victorian business chambers off Edinburgh's High Street, not unlike an atelier with weekly project design debates. Their key approach is to understand the personalities of place and of client. They seize the client's imagination and aspirations, then apply them to the location, the orientation, sun, wind, people patterns, openness, accessibility, shelter and privacy. This approach often creates unforeseen opportunities. They have a strong philosophy relating to design and materials in that there are objective rules for architecture in simplicity, boundary, rhythm and appropriateness. Colours sing and are alive. Enrichment of buildings is achieved through the slenderness of design and detail, and with the involvement of artists.

Maccreanor + Lavington Architects
London and Rotterdam

Since its establishment in 1990, the practice has worked on a number of housing and urban design commissions in Britain and the Netherlands. Most recently they completed a study commissioned by the municipality of Amsterdam for a waterfront city centre site for a high-density, mixed-use development, including 1,200 dwellings.

Assessor's comment

Gerard Maccreanor and Richard Lavington won a competition in Europan 2, and were commissioned to design a substantial housing project in Zaaneiland, Netherlands – the first building by British architects to emerge from the Europan commissioning system. The office was first set up in Rotterdam, but now has an office in London; one partner runs each office, but both colloborate on the design work for any project. The practice's work is founded on the idea of urban place-making based on rationality and appropriateness, using a modern language that takes account of context. Many of the Dutch schemes include urban design at a substantial scale and involve working with other architects. Both at urban and single-building scale, the approach is to set up a clear unifying framework which allows for flexibility and complexity to be developed.

Main picture opposite, above and right: Lux Center, new cinema complex, Hoxton Square, London. (photos: Helene Binet). Left and below: Zaaneiland housing, Holland (photos: Ann Bousema).

Mark Fisher Architects
London

Following the establishment of MFA in 1995, Mark Fisher has built on his involvement with progressive construction and environmental technology, in particular its application in the fields of transport and housing. The practice aims to provide innovative but practical design solutions to complex problems and has a commitment to the use of appropriate technologies in the pursuit of a sustainable built environment.

Assessor's comment

During ten years working for Nicholas Grimshaw & Partners, Mark Fisher was responsible for major projects including the Sainsbury supermarket in Camden and the British Pavilion at Seville. Since setting up MFA he has been involved in commercial, transport and domestic projects including a number of feasibility and masterplan studies. This is a highly professional practice with wide experience of projects in Europe and elsewhere. It provides solutions to complex situations that are both innovative and functional. Transport, housing and sustainability in general are areas of special interest, although the practice has yet to start on a new build project.

Above: proposal for sustainable housing development, Cornwall. Right: proposal for technology centre, Plymouth, Devon. Below, far left: proposal for railway station, London. Below left: retail outlet, Newcastle, for Warehouse (photo: Peter Cook).

Matthew Lloyd Architects
London

Since 1989 the practice has developed a distinctive approach to design through numerous competition entries and an involvement with teaching and academic debate. It has particular concerns about the social responsibility of architecture seeking to make its buildings democratic and accountable to the community which they serve. In addition they believe the built fabric must contribute to the wider urban and civic space it inhabits where design quality is paramount.

Assessor's comment

Matthew Lloyd's minimal budget housing association scheme in one of London's poorest areas, off Brick Lane in Bethnal Green, is next to a similar project procured by design & build methods. Theirs is much, much better. Working up to the £1 million range, the practice is committed to 'social architecture', particularly youth needs. One of eight shortlisted practices in the heavily-contested recent competition to provide a design for the refurbishment of the Hackney Empire.

Above: temporary opera house, Spitalfields, London. Far right and right: sheltered housing scheme, Brick Lane, London

Matthew Priestman Architects
London

Matthew Priestman formed the practice in 1988 after extensive experience on major commercial projects, some overseas, with well-established practices, including a £45 million office building on Canary Wharf in London's Docklands. In recent years the practice has achieved a high profile in architectural competitions on the continent, taking advantage of the more open architectural culture there. In August 1996 the firm was shortlisted as one of ten practices for the 65,000 sq m Danish State Archives. It has recently completed designs for the first phase of the University College of South Stockholm, commissioned to work in parallel with local firms of architects following an international competition. It also won first prize in the Orestaden competition, a masterplan project for the 3.5 million sq m extension to the Danish capital Copenhagen.

Assesor's comment

Matthew Priestman's success in European competitions for major academic, social and cultural projects is in marked contrast to the scale of what he has been able to build here in the UK, which is mostly domestic conversions and refurbishments, and is probably equally true of many firms of this age and experience.

    Projects in the UK under way at the moment include a refurbishment of a large house in Belgravia, central London, and the creation of a dramatic showroom space in Camden, north London for a large American building product manufacturer. In both these projects Matthew Priestman demonstrates an ability to maximise the drama available in tight spaces, to apply materials in a way that injects both logic and colour to a scheme. A practice that is clearly ready to tackle larger projects.

Main picture opposite and far left: Pembridge Mews apartment, London.
Above: University of Stockholm proposal.
Left: Copenhagen University masterplan (computer image by Sham Imaging).
Right: Cheshire Home, Hitchen, Hertfordshire, a new build project for the disabled commissioned by the Leonard Cheshire Foundation.

A. McInnes Gardner & Partners
Glasgow

Although a long-established practice – it
was founded in 1910 by Alexander McInnes
Gardner – it is now run by two young partners
Alastair MacIntyre and Stuart Begg. Historically
the firm had a reputation for the fitting out of
ships, including the Queen Mary, the Mauritania
and most notably the Royal Yacht Brittania in
association with Sir Hugh Casson. The focus
of the practice is now in the commercial sector
with industrial buildings, and areas of particular
activity in interior design and historical
refurbishment. The practice believes in relying
on the application of information technology
to traditional design skills to produce a
more effecient design and management
process that allows the client greater access
to the process.

Assessor's comment

An old established practice – best known
for working on naval interiors, now being
rejuvenated by Alastair MacIntyre. The firm's
new incarnation is based on low budget,
well-detailed work. Stylish interiors, very
competently executed and value for money.
Relatively high profile industrial work that,
like the interiors, is strong image building
and shape making.

Above, right and bottom
right: Daniel Montgomery
& Sons, new plastic moulding
factory, Kirkintilloch,
Scotland. Left, both
images: Ticket Centre,
Candleriggs, Glasgow.

MUF Architects
London

The Muf Design Team works as a collaborative practice of art and architecture. They are currently working on a number of projects implementing art and urban design embedded in the cultural and social fabric of the city. The team have taught since the late 1980s at the Architectural Association, the University of North London and Chelsea School of Art and Design, developing a body of theoretical work which, alongside built projects, has been published and exhibited internationally.

Assessor's comment

Collaborative exploratory practice that seeks to expand the social and political role of architecture by incorporating broader influences from outside. They suggest a new way for architects to make their work link into both the community and more commercial concerns. They attempt to make architecture less shallow in its concerns; often difficult to express in buildings and urban design, but absolutely necessary. Interest in their work – which includes the design of Sir Denys Lasdun's recent show at the Royal Academy and a scheme to improve Southwark Street as part of The Architecture Foundation's Future Southwark design initiative – is growing and their ideas have won, and deserved, a wide audience. They probably need to consolidate their theoretical approach with more built examples of it. They have just been given the chance with their appointment to design one of the interiors in the Millennium Dome in Greenwich.

Main picture and left: Purity and Tolerance exhibition at the Architecture Foundation, 1992. Far right: Sir Denys Lasdun Exhibition design, Royal Academy of Arts, 1997. Right: Gym, Waterloo, London.

McDowell + Benedetti
London

The practice was formed in 1996 but the two partners first collaborated in 1991 on a joint-winning scheme for the regeneration of Smithfield Market in Dublin, completed in July 1996. They met while working for Munkenbeck + Marshall; MacDowell went on to set up his own practice in 1990 and Benedetti went to work for David Chipperfield. Their new practice is working on a 100 apartment scheme on a Thames-side site in the Isle of Dogs in London's Docklands, a healthcare scheme in south London, the conversion of an office block to housing and a Jigsaw menswear store has opened in the West End. The practice was a shortlisted finalist in the Financial Times Millennium Bridge Competition for the River Thames.

Assessor's comment

The practice is strongly design-led and already has a number of notable, if small projects completed. The office enjoys a range of interesting work rapidly expanding in scale with commissions up to £10million in value plus an involvement in masterplanning a major Malaysian university campus with YRM Architects.

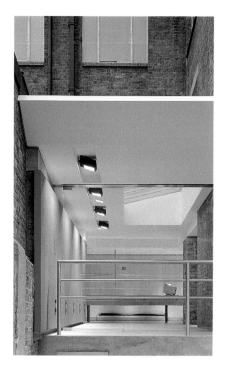

Main picture opposite, above left and left: penthouse apartment/art gallery, Oliver's Wharf, London (photo: Tim Soar). Above right: Options fashion company headquarters and showrooms, London. Below: Millennium Bridge competition entry, London (photo: Tim Soar).

Niall McLaughlin Architects
London

Niall McLaughlin Architects is a small practice with experience in cultural, community and residential buildings. Their reputation comes from an inventive use of materials based on extensive knowledge of the crafts and processes involved. They have designed objects from furniture and light fittings to whole areas of landscape. The theme that runs through all their work is light, which they consider to be the primary material of architecture. Every project is an attempt to reinvent the way in which buildings are changed by natural and artificial light.

Assessor's comment

This is a small practice which fluctuates in size according to workload. The practice has designed buildings and interiors for a range of uses including residential, recreational, community and religious. They are very aware of the relationship between a building and its setting and are inventive in the use of materials. The use of light, both natural and artificial, is used to create exciting and unexpected results. The ambition of the practice is to remain small, working on projects up to £1 million in value, designing public buildings and community projects which are carefully detailed using a wide range of materials.

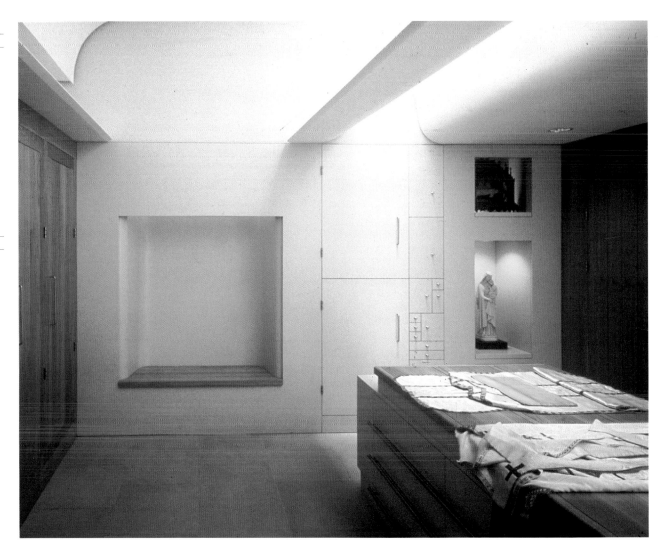

All pictures opposite and left: hide for a photographer, Foxhall, Northants.
Above: the sacristy, Carmelite Monastry, Kensington, London.
Far left: apartment, living room, Notting Hill, London.

OMI Architects
Manchester

Established in 1988, the practice's commitment to thoroughness and innovation has led to involvement in complex projects, often with buildings of historical significance, and a series of national awards. Emphasis is placed on fostering a spirit of goodwill and constructive collaboration on the part of all those involved in the design process.

Assessor's comment

With experience of a broad range of building types and, in recent years, a particular strength and reputation in Lottery-funded museum and sports buildings, this practice works closely with its clients to produce elegant buildings in response to difficult and complex sites and briefs. This non-hierarchical office is flexible in its approach and collaborative in its method of working. Models, complemented by computer graphic renderings as appropriate, are used extensively as a basis for design exploration and dialogue. The practice has a relaxed, caring approach and a reputation for quality and well-crafted buildings.

Main picture: housing and estate office, Boundary Lane, Hulme, Manchester. Far right: Pump House Museum, Manchester. Right: Manchester Business School refurbishment. Below left: adaptions to entrance hall, Canterbury House, Birmingham.

Left: detail, London College of Fashion Library. Above: London College of Printing. Below: Brune Street workshops (photo Chris Gascoigne). Below right, both images: Cochrane Theatre, Central St Martin's College, London.

Odedina & Allardyce Architects
London

Odedina & Allardyce Architects was formed in 1995, formulated on the belief that architecture is an art form and as such relates culturally and socially to the time of its creation. They have carried out a wide range of projects for an equally broad range of clients, ranging from provision of large, complex and highly specific buildings to simple, temporary shelter.

Assessor's comment

Strong colours and *objets trouvés* are often used as points of interest within a contemporary steel, wood and glass aesthetic. The work is thoughtful and competent and sometimes wilfully eclectic, playing with layering, grid and scale. Some of it feels like installations – which is not surprising given that a lot of their projects are for arty academic institutions which require economical, robust solutions that can be achieved with a minimum of on-site disruption. This demands good organisational abilities and a close relationship with client and trusted contractors. Their work for the Pegasus Theatre in Oxford (a Lottery bid) is a chance to undertake more ambitious work, building on their earlier success at the Cochrane Theatre at Central St Martin's, London. Otherwise there is no experience of new build (as a practice). Refurbishment experience, including that of historic buildings, is more extensive.

Page & Park Architects
Glasgow

The practice was formed in 1981 by David Page and Brian Park and has established expertise in a number of areas in addition to general architectural practice. Urban design and planning projects form a significant proportion of the practice's workload either as project leaders or as consultants in multi-disciplinary teams. Historic buildings and conservation also forms an important part of their work and a number of museum, visitor centre, exhibition and tourist-related projects have been undertaken – sensitively integrated with the existing environment. In recent years the practice has become heavily involved in new-build projects in Gorbals, Govan, Elderpark and at Strathclyde University.

Assessor's comment

Page & Park are one of the most distinguished of the younger generation of Scottish architects, combining a sensitive feel for issues of architectural identity and continuity with a committment to contemporary internationalism. It is clear that it is a partnership with an unusual combination of skills – both sensitive to aesthetic issues and businesslike, and enormously committed to their work.

Above: Port Glasgow Municipal Building: repair, conservation and extension to provide library and related public facilities. Right: St Francis Church, the Gorbals, Glasgow. Left: The Italian Centre, shops and offices, Glasgow. Far left: The Lighthouse project for Glasgow 1999, conservation and adaption of the former Glasgow Herald building.

Pawson Williams Architects
London

The practice was founded in 1987, since when it has specialised in cultural buildings; in particular, theatre and concert spaces, libraries, museums and galleries. It also skilled in urban design. Their endeavour is always to create a visionary architecture of clarity and distinction; a worthy, memorable place which must be a pleasure both to visit and to work in.

Assessor's comment

The two partners, Terry Pawson and Keith Williams, are of high intellect and creativity – dedicated to their profession, full of energy and a desire to succeed. They have weathered particularly difficult early years, completed a number of projects and been successful in a number of competitions. They are now well placed and ready to take on further significant work which will be dealt with in a professional, considered and creative way.

Above: main stair to Earth Galleries, and right: No.3 Foyer Gallery, Earth Galleries, Natural History Museum, London (photos: Nathan Willock).
Far right: Centre Regional de la Musique et de la Voix, Argenteuil, Paris (photo: Eamonn O'Mahoney). Left: Proposal for Technopolis scheme, Norwich (photo: Andrew Putler).

Panter Hudspith Architects
London

A wide variety of projects have been tackled since the practice was set up in 1987 by Mark Panter and Simon Hudspith. Early work focused on office refurbishments and one-off houses, but in the 1990s it widened to include art house cinemas, restaurants, health centres, school buildings and urban planning. Following the practice's participation in an exhibition at the Royal Fine Arts Commission in London called Thames Connections, it has been involved in a number of projects on the south bank of the Thames in London. On behalf of the Southwark Groundwork Trust, the practice has refurbished an area under Southwark Bridge, including engraved maps of the river, lighting and landscaping. Other recent community projects include a health centre in Stanhope, County Durham and new technology building for a grant-maintained girls' school in Kent. The practice has also recently completed the fit-out of six floors of the Centre Point office building in central London.

Assessor's comment

Although just ten years old this has the impression of a mature practice providing a safe pair of hands. Although many of the projects have been constrained by tight budgets the results have retained a clear design quality. In York they have successfully designed a new cinema complex in a very sensitive riverside environment, while in the freer planning context of Newcastle-upon-Tyne the practice has created a lively and elegant design for the Pitcher & Piano chain. Ready for bigger jobs.

Main picture opposite, left and below left: Pitcher & Piano bar and restaurant, Newcastle Quayside. Above and below right: Camera Press building, London.

Parr Shearer
Glasgow

Founded by Lucy Parr and Graeme Shearer in 1994; both studied at the Mackintosh School of Architecture, Glasgow. They worked together during the ten years prior to setting up practice, including the restoration and modernisation of their own flat in Glasgow's Park Circus area, which was featured in Glasgow's successful bid for the title UK City of Architecture and Design 1999, and was awarded the Sponsors' Prize by the Glasgow Institute of Architects.

Assessor's comment

Ambitious and committed, although realised work to date is small-scale and mainly based on interior remodelling. Carried out the refurbishment of spectacular high Victorian tenement flat in Glasgow for their own use, which combined painstaking recreation of period detail – gold leaf and all – with a suave modern insertion at mezzanine level. More interested in the intricacies of spatial manipulation than in history. Their Offices for Glasgow 1999 was also ingenious.

Main picture: Christies International, Scotland. Below and below right: offices for Glasgow 1999 (photo: Keith Hunter). Far right: People's Palaces exhibition (photo: Keith Hunter). Left: Parr Shearer home, Glasgow (photo: Chris Gascoigne, View).

Procter:Rihl
London

Procter:Rihl is a young multi-disciplinary practice focused on furniture and architecture with special interests in environment and energy studies, housing and exhibition design. The practice has been working with concepts of folding, layering, transparency, lamination and patterns, primarily within two design disciplines of contrasting scales – furniture and architecture.

Assessor's comment

Although they haven't built much yet, they are clearly a coming force. Stylistically innovative, curvy and colourful, drawing inspiration from the fashionable interest in the modernism of the 50s and 60s. In their case, the partners are particularly interested in the Brazilian landscape artist Roberto Burle Marx, with his Miróesque use of colours and shapes. Their innovative furniture design is rapidly winning them customers for apartment refurbishment work and a market presence. A practice that shows a lot of promise.

Above and right: Soho penthouse, London. Far right: exhibition stand for Blueprint magazine at 100% Design show, London. Left: detail of furniture design.

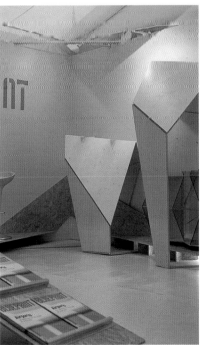

Patel Taylor
London

Both partners worked with leading practice MacCormac Jamieson and Prichard before setting up Patel Taylor in 1989. Based in their self-designed studio in Camden, the ten-strong practice's work encompasses a broad range of projects from sensitive conversions, studios, public buildings, education buildings and large landscape projects such as the Thames Barrier Park – and a correspondingly broad range of clients in the public and private sectors. The practice has prepared masterplans, urban designs and development guidelines for projects throughout Europe including redevelopment and infrastructure projects in Scotland, a prestigious city centre site near Reims Cathedral and an environmental, urban and economic appraisal for the town of Chateauroux in mid-France. Several projects have been won through international design competitions.

Assessor's comment

A well-established practice with a lively palette of sensitive materials. Particularly adroit at inserting new uses into sensitive historical structures and sites, yet thoroughly contemporary. Seasoned competition entrants, but now moving into the serious commissions arena. They possess a tangible design edge over more established practices which stems from their thorough analysis and understanding of urban design issues. This has fostered a strategic approach to establishing the key issues in projects of whatever scale or type, down to using detailed forms for each room in a scheme. A cool, clean, modern style incorporating natural materials with a highly sensitive feel for maximising space, light and utility. An outstanding practice.

Main picture opposite: Arts centre and gallery, Treuddyn, near Mold, Wales.
Left and above right: The practice's own office in Camden, London.
Right: Thames Barrier Park visitors centre.

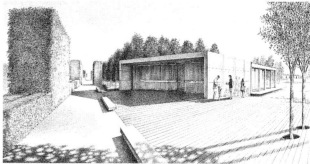

Perkins Ogden Architects
Alresford, Hampshire

Mervyn Perkins and Mark Ogden formed the practice in January 1987. They have a wide experience of projects in the leisure, community and education fields and are emerging as an architectural practice of national prominence following their double success in the 1996 RIBA Awards. They have been involved in more than 30 projects in the education sector alone with a joint construction value approaching £50million.

Assessor's comment

Friendly and committed practice with a strong and successful track record in publicly-funded projects, predominantly in the education sector. They take a multi-tasking approach to projects which is non-hierarchical, with one partner and one architect responsible for each project. They are well organised and very efficient, and work with other practices when other skills or higher levels of resources are required. The partners are very involved with projects, rather than being tied up with management. The practice aims to provide 'robust architectural solutions' which are cost effective, on time and within budget.

Main picture opposite and above right: Greene King plc, new brewery distribution depot, Hampshire (photos: Adrian Harvey). Left: Sparsholt College, Hampshire, new library and information centre (photo: Adrian Harvey). Below: Norsebury House, private residence, pool enclosure and sauna (photo: Matthew Weinreb).

Peter Barber Architects
London

Peter Barber Architects was established in 1989 in studios they built on a canalside wharf in London's East End. The office has a portfolio of projects in Europe and the Middle East, including a number of innovative residential schemes and award-winning planning studies commissioned by the Cities of Warsaw and Berlin. They have more recently been involved in ecological projects and inner city regeneration in London.

Assessor's comment

This practice has a small but enviable reputation for innovative thinking and its commitment to radical solutions and excellence in design. Its portfolio covers a surprisingly wide geographic spread, including Botswana, Athens and eastern Europe, and most notably in Saudi Arabia where the widely-published Villa Anbar was shortlisted for the Aga Khan Award. Less well known is the fact that the practice has a 100 per cent success rate with local grant applications for architectural projects. The practice has respected strengths in masterplanning based on its work in Warsaw and Berlin and has recently taken on replanning Broadway Market and masterplanning Thames Valley University.

Main picture opposite and below right: Villa Anbar, Saudi Arabia. Above and left: Q studio. Far left: Andrews Wharf, London.

Far left and below: Fruitmarket Gallery, Edinburgh. Left and below right: 17 Royal Terrace Mews, Edinburgh. All pictures opposite: house, Gilmour Road, Edinburgh.

Richard Murphy Architects
Edinburgh

Richard Murphy Architects was founded in October 1991 and the practice is well known for its renovation of the Fruitmarket Gallery in Edinburgh, completed in 1993 for which it won an RIBA Award. Murphy has also completed a cancer care centre for the Western General Hospital in the city and an office conversion and fit out for the Royal Fine Art Commission of Scotland. Murphy was a full-time lecturer in design at Edinburgh University and has worked for the respected practices of MacCormac Jamieson & Pritchard and Alsop Lyall & Störmer

Assessor's comment

This high-profile office in an Edinburgh shop, with windows full of models, is run like a busy atelier. It has had unusual success in competitions and awards (the only UK practice to be twice shortlisted for the Stirling prize), which attests to a popularity that appeals to both clients and architects alike. Particular practice focus is on the 'essential enjoyment of a building': what clients can contribute to design, qualities of orientation and internal light, and clarity of detail. They aspire to make buildings kinetic, able to change to a different architectural expression to accommodate differing social functions, times of day or year. The language emerges from how that is achieved. They particularly enjoy transforming existing buildings and have an overriding belief in reinforcing what is there and recovering what has been lost.

Russell Light Architectural Design
Sheffield

Since 1988, Russell Light has worked on a series of domestic-scale projects in the Peak District National Park which have been built using craft-based techniques. He began working with Gary Thomason in 1994 and they have just completed their first joint competition entry. Current projects include a barn conversion at Stoney Middleton, Derbyshire and a house extension at Totley, Sheffield.

Assessor's Comment

Russell Light is a full-time lecturer at Sheffield University who possesses highly developed design and critical skills. Recent projects have been built by developer/contractors following the sketch designs and models prepared by Russell. Care in design and understanding of design issues are a strength. The practice's management and production information side is in a formative stage.

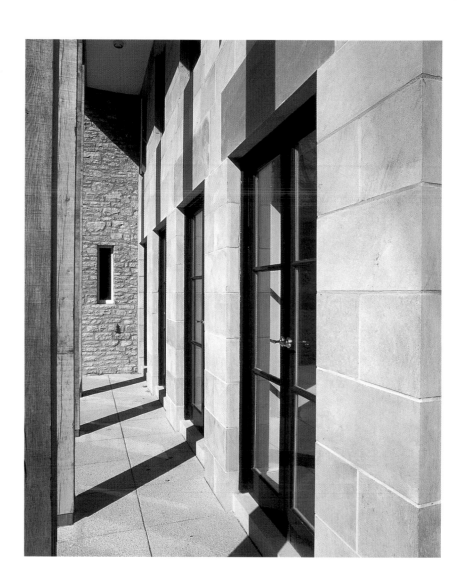

Main picture opposite, above and left: The Orchard, Calver, Derbyshire. Far left: Mitchell Field Farm, Hathersage, Derbyshire.

Sarah Wigglesworth Architects
London

Sarah Wigglesworth Architects aspire to build using everyday, readily available materials assembled into imaginative and innovative structures which can be achieved with modest means and for low maintenance costs. The practice has designed cultural buildings, offices, houses, public housing schemes and structures for education, dance and sport.

Comment

Wigglesworth manages to explore new ideas in sustainability and ecological economy without resorting to a bulky, handicrafted aesthetic. Instead a humanistic modernism which uses everyday materials in an innovative way is key in developing an 'urban vernacular of the commonplace'. Complexity of space and a rich syntax is more important than structural gymnastics in what is a synthesis of the green and a committed organism. The practice works hard at bringing together the academic and the practical, the hi-tech and the low-tech. Work is, at present, small scale, but the practice appears to be on the cusp of taking on more complex and extensive new build projects.

Right, left and far right: house in Chelsea, London (photos: Jonathan Law). Below: model shot, proposed house and office, north London.

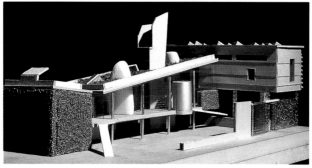

Stan Bolt set up in practice as a sole practitioner in 1993 and has rapidly developed a reputation for producing modern innovative design for congenial living and working spaces in environmentally sensitive areas. Although the practice is based in south Devon – in premises designed by the practice – work has been undertaken all over the UK. It has included additional space for The New School in Exminster and an annexe to 7 Plymouth Road, Totnes and both these projects won Royal Institute of British Architects Regional Awards. He has also designed an office extension for pharmaceutical conglomerate Zeneca.

Assessor's comment

Stan Bolt works strictly within the well-tried limits of his own experience without being prosaic. Nothing is left to chance and there is an air of excellence both in the office itself and in the completed work. Clients and buildings are handled with care and skill. Although the projects have been modest in scale up to now, it is clear that, such is the success of the practice, commissions are getting larger. Because of this, the practice will be moving into bigger premises to be shared with the two technicians who work with the office from time to time, both on CAD and on general technological matters.

Above: additional accommodation to the New School, New School, Exminster Below and right: annexe to private house, Totnes.

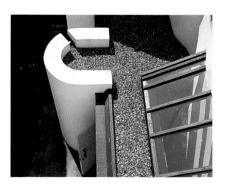

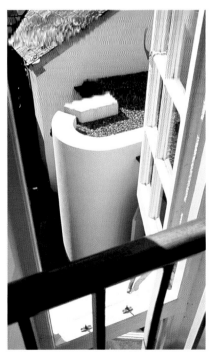

Sauerbruch Hutton Architects
London and Berlin

Led by Louisa Hutton and Matthias Sauerbruch, the practice has established a high design profile through its project and competition work since its foundation in 1989. Although the Berlin office is larger than the London one, the partners regard London as their main base; however, they consider their practice a single entity and computer links mean that information can be exchanged effortlessly. The office is regularly invited to contribute to exhibitions in many countries, and has had a number of individual shows.

Assessor's comment

The practice successfully achieves a flow of staff and ideas between its two offices. The London office, although the smaller, is efficiently run and well-equipped. A range of projects, from house conversions in Central London to the GSW headquarters building in Berlin, have been completed or are under construction. The practice adopts a very individual approach to projects, working with the client to ensure that the building is easy to occupy and economic in use of energy while creating a thrilling environment. To quote the partners, they are 'guided by the modern instinct of "wanting to make reality work" indulging at the same time in the sensuality of materials and colour.' Projects show an ability to use existing buildings in a positive way and the use of space, colour, materials and light creates truly exciting buildings that work.

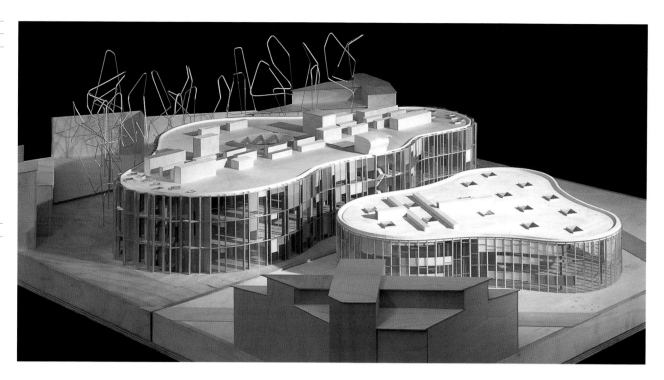

Main picture opposite: conversion of a 1960s residence, Kensington, London (photo: Helene Binet). Far left: conversion of a Victorian house, London (photo: Helene Binet). Left: extension to a headquarters building, Kreuzberg, Berlin (photo: Lepkowski + Hillman), Above: Laboratories, workshops, production facilities and offices, Berlin (photo: Lepkowski + Hillman).

Saville Jones Architects
Worthing, West Sussex

Saville Jones is a young practice, founded on solid experience and a shared enthusiasm for good architecture and drawing on its experience in leisure, housing, entertainment, ecclesiastical and commercial projects. The practice is geared to the needs of the 21st century and aware that, without squandering resources, structures can be created to meet the immediate needs of the client and respond to changing conditions during its life span. A growing awareness of environmental issues leads to a greater concern for the entire performance of a building – energy consumption, the users' enjoyment and the respect it shows for the environment.

Comment

The two partners, who came from separate local practices, have been together for four years and have concentrated on the sport and leisure sector, as far as the Channel Islands and, more recently, Gibraltar. They are appropriately organised for a small practice and make full use of their CAD resources. They demonstrate a genuine sense of accountability to clients, borne out by the number of repeat commissions.

They have received an architectural and environmental award from the Royal Borough of Windsor, as well as good coverage in both the technical and lay press. Resources allowing, they engage in competitions; they were premiated for an international ideas competition in the Channel Islands.

Main picture opposite: refurbishment of the listed Southern Pavilion, Worthing Pier (photo: Haydn Jones). Above: Magnet Leisure Centre, Maidenhead (photo: Bill Philip). Far left and left: Les Quennevais Swimming Centre, Jersey (photo: Haydn Jones).

Shed KM
Liverpool

Shed KM was formed in June 1997 from the merger of two prominent north west practices, Shed and King McAllister. Both practices have developed good reputations for innovation across a wide range of projects. Shed have produced a string of award-winning, high profile and highly successful urban renewal projects. King McAllister had good experience in the competition and exhibition world, and a series of award-winning buildings for the University of Liverpool. The new practice is currently working on a study for the Bold Street/Duke Street development area and The Match Factory, the redevelopment of the 1926 eight acre Bryant & May site next to Liverpool airport.

Assessor's comment

Post-post modern design that is witty, colourful and functional in a robust urban style is the hallmark of Shed KM's highly effective work that has in the recent past breathed new life into the centre of Liverpool. The practice is pretty unique in terms of its close links with the best-named developer to emerge in recent times, Urban Splash. This link has provided a portfolio of work that architects of a similar age group would give their eye-teeth for, both in terms of budget size and in concept. The recent merger with King McAllister should add useful further layers of design skills, experience and ideas. Rapidly emerging as one of the leading regional practices.

Left: the Ricci fashion shop. Below left, right and main picture: the Concert Square scheme in central Liverpool with bars, restaurants, cafes and offices.

Snell Associates
London

Snell Associates were formed in 1993 following completion of the new £22.6 million Opera House at Glyndebourne for Michael Hopkins & Partners, on which Robin Snell acted as project architect. In 1995 they won the RIBA international design competition for the Northern Architecture Centre in Newcastle-upon-Tyne, a showcase exhibition facility.

Assessor's comment

In 1993 Robin Snell left Michael Hopkins & Partners where he had been an associate since 1987. His final project for them – a fabric-roofed extension to the Hopkins' office building – was completed by the new practice and became a manifesto of his office's approach. Snell has adopted many of Hopkins' ways of working – including the systems used for running jobs in the office. The practice focuses on a detailed interest in the way things are put together, in a rigour in detailing and an understanding of materials. They are also interested in maximising transparency of buildings – both in terms of light and accessibility.

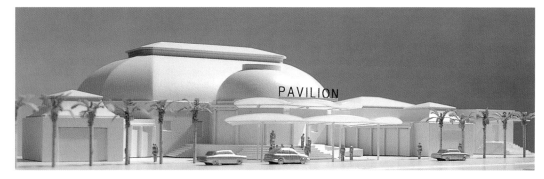

Main picture opposite: Michael Hopkins & Partners office entrance, London. Above: Winning entry for the Royal Institute of British Architects' international design competition for a Northern Architecture Centre, Newcastle-upon-Tyne. Left: Pavilion Theatre, Worthing Pier, West Sussex. Below left: Art gallery, Surrey Institute of Art and Design.

Spencer Fung Architects
London

The practice was founded in 1990 after Spencer Fung won the first prize in a competition for an apartment building in Fukuoka, Japan and has been involved in projects in the UK, Spain, China, Japan and Morocco, including a commercial development and public space in Beijing and a hotel refurbishment in Morocco. It also won an invited competition for the headquarters of the Designers Guild in London and the practice was selected to exhibit in the New British Architecture Exhibition at The Architecture Foundation in 1994. Current projects are a shop for a jewellery designer in London, an office building in the Barbican the City of London and penthouses and a private house in Kensington. Spencer Fung is designing and producing a collection of furniture. He won first prize in the 1987 RIBA International Student Competition and was an associate at David Chipperfield Architects.

Assessor's comment

This practice provides minimalistic design of great style. Domestic, commercial and retail interiors use space, light and colour to maximise the full potential of the project. Eastern influence is clear in the serenity and warmth which combines with excitement and meticulous attention to detail. The range of furniture and display fittings, which has been developed for homes and for the Joseph shops, is spare and elegant. This is very much a hands-on practice with the creativity carried through to the minutiae of craft finishes on site.

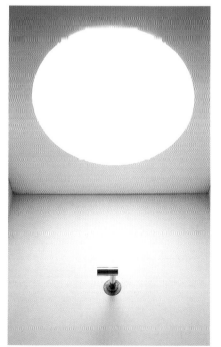

Main picture opposite and left: York House penthouse Kensington, London. Above. Designers Guild headquarters, North Kensington (photos: Peter Cook). Below and right: house in Belsize Park, London (photos: Richard Bryant, Arcaid).

Stephen Donald Architects Ltd
London

Although Stephen Donald has worked on a diverse collection of project types and scales, ranging from new-build public housing to small one-off retail outlets, his main body of work and reputation has been based on the relatively large number of music venues, cafes and bar projects. The practice has developed a methodology based on a concept of resuscitation, whereby a building which may have become programmatically, culturally or socially obsolete, can be given a new life as a consequence of contemporary architectural intervention.

Assessor's comment

Stephen Donald's two principal jobs at present are the conversion of the NatWest bank site under Centre Point in central London (a post-war listed building) into a restaurant and the Gamelan Music Project for the Deaf in Manchester. It would seem the architecture will continue to be weighty. Concrete is ubiquitous, often polished and crafted, but sometimes gouged and stressed. Strong colours prevail. The robust architecture reflects the fact that many of the projects have been in the hard-wearing end of the leisure market - clubs, music venues, etc.

Above and below right: proposed cafe/bar, Oxford Street, London.
Left: The Cube Bar, Finchley Road, London.

Studio 8 Architects
London

Main partner C J Lim graduated from the
Architectural Association, London in 1987.
He lectures at the Bartlett, University College
London and University of North London and is
currently visiting professor at the Stadelschule,
Frankfurt. He established Studio 8 Architects
in 1994.

Assessor's comment

The practice is run from C J Lim's London flat
and has been involved in a large number of
exhibitions and competitions – winning the
international competition for a cultural centre
at Univeristy College London, a 'virtual jukebox'.
The scheme is in development stages pending
an application for Arts Council lottery funding.
Studio 8 are also working as collaborators on
another application for lottery funding – a
roller-hockey stadium in Stratford, East
London, and has completed its first built
project, the fit-out of the SW Sushi Bar in
Kensington. The practice is interested in
speculative work, arts, fashion and paintings,
subterfuge and intrigue. Their designs are
largely developed from semi-abstract models
and transformed into architectural forms.
Intangible elements like light, steam or various
kinds of movement are used to animate the
resulting building design – often providing a
'free' addition to a tight budget. Competitions
play a large part in the practice's work.

Above and left: computer
images of interior,
SW Sushi Bar, London.
Below right: computer image,
proposed UCL Cultural
Centre. Below: computer
Rear elevation, UCL
Museum proposal.

Studio BAAD
Hebden Bridge, West Yorkshire

Studio BAAD was established by Philip Bintliff to provide high quality, innovative design skills. In 1994 Ray Phillips, formerly partner in architects Cullearn and Phillips joined Studio BAAD. His background and experience of large projects contributed significantly to the management, design, technical and technological development of the practice.

Studio BAAD have an established track record of collaborating with artists on a wide variety of projects. This ranges from artists' involvement on two buildings for Simon Jersey and culminated recently in an appointment by Warrington Borough Council to assist with its bid for Arts Lottery funding for a town centre project. Following a series of commercial and industrial new build and interior design projects, Studio BAAD established a Healthcare Design Group reflecting a growing workload for healthcare clients and to combine an abiding interest in technical aspects of design and construction with innovative design.

Assesor's comment

A happy office sharing one space on the top floor of a converted mill. Design work and draughtsmanship are of a high standard. The approach to a brief is good and the architectural response reflects the care taken. Philip Bintliff is obviously the driving force and the staff respond well to his 'hands-on' approach. The office could cope with large schemes – management resources are suitable.

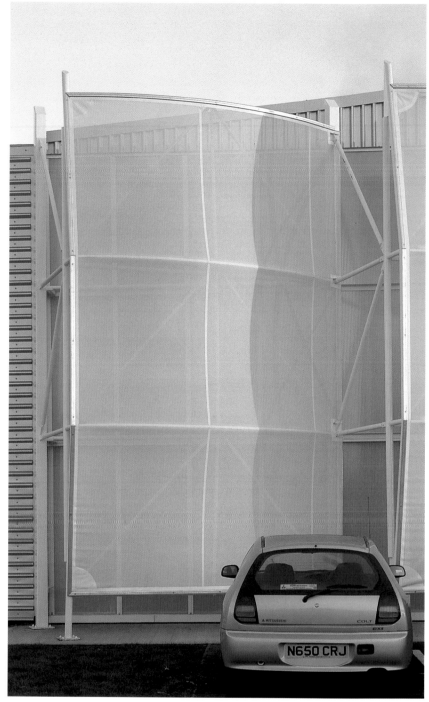

Above: Simon Jersey 2 headquarters, Accrington, sunshades. Main picture opposite: sun shades at night. Left: Simon Jersey Headquarters, Accrington. Far left: both shots KP foods, Teeside, glass supported canopy. All photos: Jeremy Cockayne.

Sergison Bates Architects
London

The practice has won prizes in several international competitions for public buildings and urban scale developments, and has been the subject of a number of exhibitions. Both partners have lectured and written papers on architecture and their work has been published in the UK and abroad. Recent projects include an office refurbishment in Clerkenwell, London, and a craft studio in Bridport, Dorset.

Assessor's comment

Sergison Bates are a young practice whose work is directed towards a broad range of social and public projects. Good organisation and professionalism is combined with an attitude that is positive, sharp and thinking. Having first worked with other successful practices, both partners have a critical approach and enjoy working with 'enlightened' clients so that their projects are the result of collaboration. A rational approach to form is combined with an investigative and imaginative use of materials.

Above: Windmill Montessori Nursery School, London (photo: Dennis Gilbert). Right: new pub, Walsall. Left and far left: warehouse apartment, London (photo: Alan Williams).

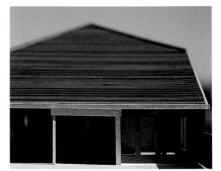

The practice was formed in 1992 and its workload is varied. Many of the projects are within sensitive landscaped environments or urban contexts of historical or architectural importance. They have design advisor specialisation for the re-imaging of buildings and services and in 1996 Craig Downie was appointed as a design advisor for the new Heathrow second terminal project. The Studio is also an approved London Docklands Development Corporation consultant. Clients have included the French Treasury in London, government departments, BAA-Lynton and the West London Training and Enterprise Council.

Assessor's comment

Since Studio Downie began four years ago, their workload has included refurbishments of historical and architecturally sensitive buildings/sites, interior design, new buildings, furniture, landscape design and graphics in a variety of commercial, private and public projects. Their accolades include competition work and international publication and exhibitions.

Above and left: Hat Hill Sculpture Gallery, Goodwood, Sussex. Left is the gallery's educational classroom. Far left and right: Southall Opportunities Centre, west London.

All images: offices for Radius Design Consultants Parkway, Richmond upon Thames. All photos Paul Tyagi.

Studio MG Architects
London

The two partners, Craig Moffat and John Grimes have over 11 years' experience working in London, Paris and Amsterdam. Their project range covers low budget residential commissions to high profile, high budget corporate projects.

Assessor's comment

John Grimes and Craig Moffat formed Studio MG in 1995 having both taught at the Macintosh School of Architecture, Glasgow, where they won a competition for a sports centre in Paris. The practice is small but enthusiastic, combining a strong design sense with a pragmatic understanding of clients' needs and project realities. Professional and management skills will grow with the practice. It currently enjoys a range of small commissions which are approached with panache.

Main picture, left and far left: Rayham Barn, Whitstable, Kent. Right: Timothy Taylor Gallery, London.

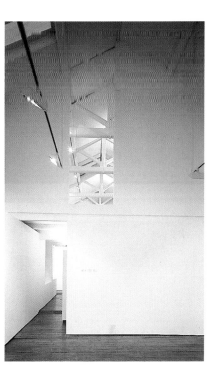

Thomas Croft Architect
London

Thomas Croft Architect was established as a practice in 1995 although Croft has undertaken many private projects from 1987 onwards. The practice's early work has often involved the reuse of historic listed structures in a contemporary manner. Rayham Barn in Kent and the Timothy Taylor Gallery in London are good examples of this approach.

Assessor's Comment

The practice specialises in providing exciting and playful buildings for discerning institutions. Projects include renovations and extensions to historic building and building within locations requiring delicate intervention. Solutions are seen as a simple expression of the client's brief, placed in context of the surroundings. Modern forms are informed by the situation.

Experience with major contemporary architects — Richard Meier, Rick Mather and John Pawson, provides knowledge of cutting-edge materials and construction methods, together with that of period interior design and detailing.

The practice tends to work with the same client on more than one project, and to continue monitoring project through their in-life use. A competent all-round architect who seems to be operating within his capacity whilst wishing to spread his wings.

The Architects Practice
London

The Architects Practice was set up in 1986 as an intentionally small design-led firm by Simon Foxell, who is responsible for all the practice's designs as well as the process of building them. The practice has a strong belief in the act of building and the poetry of modern architecture. Its designs try to explore and express the nature of materials, recently working extensively with glass and timber, to generate a quietly expressive architecture.

Assessor's comment

Simon Foxell works closely with reputable engineers to produce innovative small buildings which, in particular, explore the properties of glass and timber. Properly detailed timber frames without being vernacular, and cutting-edge glazing technology allow continuity while expressing the contemporary. The rigorous but sensitive results have led to a number of successful interventions in historic buildings. The size of projects and practice guarantees close partner involvement in the schemes.

Opposite, above and below:
Exercise Pavilion, Highgate.
north corner, far right, pool
house, front elevation,
Hillgate, north London.
All photos: Peter Cook.

Vaughan & McIlhenny Architects
Fortrose, Aberdeen

Following a period working for a series of practices in London, Lucy Vaughan and Peter McIlhenny decided to return to the north of Scotland in late 1993 when they set up their new practice. The practice is committed to improving the prevalent rural building idiom in rural Scotland through greater reference to context, composition and detail and to bringing life back to abandoned, but inherently beautiful and appropriate buildings. Nearly 20 projects have been tackled in the last four years ranging in budget from £10,000 to £2.5 million. The largest project under way is the £2.5 million renovation of the 19th century fishery town at Lower Pulteney, Wick. Other projects include art galleries, houses, extensions, conversions, playgroup premises and hotel alterations.

Assessor's comment

Vaughan & McIlhenny in Fortrose, Aberdeen, are a small practice and the two partners have previous experience working in a range of small and large practices on a broad spectrum of work, all with a high design profile. Their high design ambition, combined with ability, is fairly rare in northern Scotland.

This promising young practice will certainly carry out some very good work given the opportunity and win awards in the future.

Left and far right: housing at Holcroft Road, Hackney, London. Above: Nsoromma House, residential therapy centre, south London. Top Left: 'folding flat', apartment for a Reuters correspondent, the kitchen, north London.

Walter Menteth + Graeme Little Architects
London

A practice which has designed public and private housing, community centres and multi-purpose halls, music and creche facilities, mental health hostels, workshop, office and retail developments and tackled urban planning, regeneration and site development strategies. Of particular interest to the partners are energy efficient strategies, innovative building technologies, community liaison and inner-city, post-industrial sites. Current projects include eight flats for disabled users in Battersea, private homes in Dominica and Jamaica, the reorganisation of courtyards within a 1970s Wandsworth high-rise estate and a mental health group home in Newham.

Assessor's comment

An efficient small practice founded in 1993 and involved in interesting buildings using advanced energy conservation techniques. Its experience to date covers a wide range of building types to which has been applied imaginative and practical architectural solutions. The firm's buildings are characterised by simple clear geometry and an innovative use of materials.

Established in 1993, projects range from complex public buildings to small residential projects located both in the UK and abroad with experience of arts and sports lottery-funded schemes. They won the international competition to design an art gallery for the KwaZulu Natal Society of Arts in Durban, South Africa in 1995, which was completed in 1996. Recent projects include new facilities for Hendon Rugby Club, London, a beach house in Tobago, new apartments and houses in London and three Jigsaw day nurseries, in Leicester, in Bristol and at Stockley Park near Heathrow, London.

Assessor's comment

Both Cindy Walters and Michal Cohen are from South Africa. Their employees and jobs tend to be from many different countries, giving them an approach which draws on varied sources and provides considerable client experience. They have no particular design slogans, but are interested in maximum flexibility – so their buildings can easily accommodate different uses and changes in climate – in maximising budget, in natural ventilation and green issues, and in developing a modern language from indigenous vernacular cultures specific to the particular building and site.

Main picture: Art loft, KwaZulu Natal Society of Arts Gallery, Durban, South Africa.
Above: House extension, north west London. Right: Jigsaw, Day Nursery, Bristol.
All photos Dennis Gilbert.

Wells MacKereth Architects
London

Wells Mackereth was set up in 1995 by James Wells and Sally Mackereth, who have both previously worked on a wide range of projects while working for leading architects and designers. Work to date includes the Polygon Bar and Grill in Clapham, and two loft-style apartment fit outs, also in London. The practice is interested in combining materials, colours, texture and light to create abstract settings and intriguing spaces. A set design for leading contemporary dance choreographer Bunty Matthias at the Queen Elizabeth Hall received critical acclaim in the press.

Assessor's comment

Wells Mackereth is well organised and has produced varied high quality work. The practice's smaller work has received good press coverage. They are known for residential work and they have a particular interest in in theatre set design and exhibition work. Early days, but recommended.

Top: Soho loft apartment.
(Photo Chris Gascoigne).
Left and right: all images
Polygon Bar and Grill,
London SW4 (Photos:
Michael Mack).

Woolf Architects
London

Jonathan Woolf began his own practice in
1999 with the widely-published project for the
Ijaz apartment. At the same time he won first
prizes in two international design competitions,
one for an urban regeneration scheme in
Dublin, the other a design for an office furniture
system for the the next century. These set
out the basis for a substantial body of 15
built projects, both residential and commercial,
and urban regeneration competitions including
a project for speculative terraced housing
in Manchester, featured recently on a
Channel 4 documentary on the themes of
new urban regeneration.

Assessor's comment

An impressive portfolio of striking apartment
refurbishments and a competition-winning
urban design project to reclaim a run-down
Georgian square in Dublin languishing as a
car park and intermittent horse market. A very
controlled neo-modernism that works with the
character of existing buildings, finds a quirk
and then builds on it using modern materials.

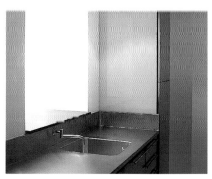

Above: Ijaz apartment,
London (photo: Matthew
Weinreb). Far right: detail of
aluminium staircase, Jonivin
Daniel Funnington Bank
Court. Left and right: interior
details, Carmel Court
(photos: Etienne Clement).

Zombory-Moldovan Moore
London

Expertise has been developed in designing for the arts; for arts organisations, collectors, artists. The practice has also established itself as designers of restaurants and internationally as specialist retail architects. They practice exploits the potential of materials, light and space to create buildings which are rich, inspiring settings for modern life. Projects include a feasibility study for a Chinese cultural centre, galleries and residence for a private art collection in London, theatre design for five new plays, new auction rooms for Sotheby's in London and a 3000 sq m studio and workshop scheme for artists, crafstpeople and designers, also in London.

Assessor's comment

The practice was started in 1990 by Adam Zombory-Moldovan, who runs a post-graduate studio at Cambridge University, and Rowan Moore, the architectural writer. Today, Moore acts as a consultant to the practice; Zombory-Moldovan maintains his link with teaching which he sees as an important contribution to the character of the practice. Two other members of the practice also teach. They boast strong practical skills and a firm approach to design.

Above: Himalayan department at Spink's fine art dealers, London.
Top left: Sam Fogg art and book dealer, London. Top right: offices at Bleeding Heart Yard, London for Harring Miles Associates, publicity company. Bottom left: shoe store New Delhi. Bottom right: Carnevale restaurant, London.

Below and below right: Tree, performance structure, Glasgow. Far right: redesign of area around the Mersey Tunnel entrance, Liverpool. Right: Transformations on the edge project in Fossil for Hawthorn Housing Co-op.

Zoo Architects
Glasgow

The office generates a contemporary architecture through a continuing exploration of form, colour, functional, social and behavioural issues. There is a commitment to energy-consciousness and new technologies. The office uses environmentally-friendly products where appropriate, from sustainable sources, and materials that have low-embodied energy factors. The practice has worked on several warehouse conversions, street sculpture, and is working on a public space scheme at the entrance to the Mersey Tunnel in Liverpool.

Assessor's comment

Zoo Architects have recently won a competition to remodel the Tramway, the challenging Glasgow performance venue, and have completed the design of one of the show apartments in developer Andrew Wadsworth's Glasgow loft development, the Todd Building. Zoo reflect Glasgow's interest in an architecture of ideas – combined with experience gained with other practices, before they set up their own studio, of the realities of building.

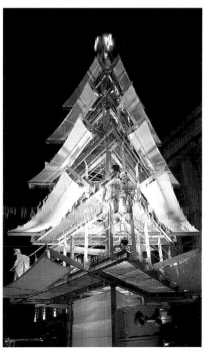

Appendix 1

A

Adjaye and Russell Architecture & Design
24 Sunbury Workshops
Swanfield Street
London E2 7LF
T: 0171 739 4969
F: 0171 739 3484
E: adjaye@compuserve.com

Resources
2 senior partners, 5 architectural staff,
1 office manager.
CAD facilities.

Largest project value to date
£500,000.

Professional indemnity
Yes.

Selected projects
Selfridges, feasibility study to remodel rear
of store,1997.
Chain of snack bars, first project Exmouth
Market, London, on site 1997.
Private house refurbishment, St John's Wood,
London, on site 1997.
Church and complex of classrooms and
houses, Atomic Hills, Ghana, 1996.
Soba, Japanese noodle bar, Poland Street,
Soho, London,1995.
Private house, Poole, extension and new house
within grounds, planning received 1995.

Awards/competitions
Lewes Ideas Competition, 1994.
Phoenix Memoria Competition, 1993,
highly commended.

Further reading
RIBA Interiors, Sept 1996.
Blueprint, April 1996.

AEM
80 O'Donnell Court
Brunswick Centre
Brunswick Square
London WC1N 1NX
T: 0171 713 9191
F: 0171 713 9199

Resources
2 architects, 4 architectural staff
CAD facilities.

Largest project value to date
£4.2 million.

Professional indemnity
Yes.

Selected projects
Kensington Bowl, new-build bowling alley,
London, £2.5 million, planning stage, 1997.
Community Music East, teaching and post-
production studios, Norwich, £900,000,
planning stage, 1997.
Swans Nest, addition to a Cotswold cottage,

Middle Chedworth, £200,000,
planning stage, 1997.
Hi Sushi, sushi bar and restaurant, London W1
£100,000, 1997.
Clanricade Gardens, residential refurbishment,
London W2, £100,000, 1995-6.
200 Shepherds Bush Road, office
development, London, £4.2 million, under
construction.

Awards/competitions
RIBA Competitions 1997, runner up.
RIBA Regional Award 1997, shortlisted.
RIBA Competitions 1995, exhibited entry.
RIBA Regional Award 1994, shortlisted.

Further reading
RIBA Interiors, June 1997.
Building Design Interiors, Autumn 1997.
New Civil Engineer, Sept 1997.
Architects' Journal, Sept1997.
Living Design Exhibition book.
RIBA/The British Council, Sept 1997.
Architects' Journal, May 9 1996.

Alastair Howe Architect
50 Tanners Way
Hunsdon Ware
Herts. SG12 8QF
T: 01279 843936
F: 01279 843937

Resources
Sole architect, staff employed as necessary.

Largest project to date
£130,000.

Professional indemnity
Yes.

Selected projects
Conversion of shop to residence, Islington,
London, £35,000, 1994-5.
New house, Hertfordshire, £57,000, 1995.
Glass-roofed bathroom extension in listed
Georgian terrace, Islington, London, £30,000,
1995-6.
Remodelling of flat, Notting Hill, London,
£75,000, 1996-7.

Awards/competitions
Europan 3, 1993.
Karlsruhe, 1992.

Exhibitions
RIBA First Sight Exhibition, 1995.
Marble Arch, 1994.

Further reading
Architecture Today, June 1996.
Build It Magazine, May 1996.
Ideal Home, August 1997.
RIBA Journal, Nov 1996.

Allan Murray Architects Limited
9 Harrison Gardens
Edinburgh EH11 1SJ
T: 0131 313 1999
F: 0131 313 1666

Resources
7 staff, including architects, landscape
architects and technical staff.
AutoCAD facilities.

Largest project value to date
£16.6 million.

Professional indemnity
Yes.

Selected projects
The MacRobert Arts Centre, Stirling,
£12.6 million, 1996.
Visions, John Logie Baird Centre, Glasgow,
£3.5 million, 1993.
Peterhead Maritime Heritage Centre,
Peterhead, £1.4 million, 1995.
Coalhill, Leith, Edinburgh, mixed-use urban
development, £3 million, 1996.

Awards/competitions
Hamilton Arts Centre, Hamilton, competition,
1997, winner.
West Side Plaza, Edinburgh, competition,
1997, winner.
Caledonia House, Edinburgh, competition,
1997, winner.

Exhibitions
1997, Contemporary Architects In Scotland,
Matthew Architecture Gallery.
1996, Water In The City: Myth & Technology,
RIAS Edinburgh Festival Exhibition.
1996, Architecture On The Horizon,
RIBA, London.

Allford Hall Monaghan Morris Architects
2nd Floor
Block B
Moorelands
5-23 Old Street
London EC1V 9HL
T: 0171 251 5261
F: 0171 251 5123

Resources
4 partners, 3 senior architects, 2 architects,
6 architectural assistants and 3 admin. staff.
CAD and computer-modelling software.

Largest project value to date
£4.2 million.

Professional indemnity
Yes.

Selected projects
Arts Centre, Edge Hill University, £2 million
lottery bid, 1997.
Great Notley Sustainable Primary School,
Essex, Phase 1, £1million, 1997.

House, Kenwood, London, £1.35 million, 1997.
Car Showroom, Warrington, £580,000, 1997.
Centro Bus Station, Walsall, £4.2 million, 1995-9.

Awards/competitions
RIBA Awards 1996 for Poolhouse, Wiltshire.

Exhibitions
Royal Academy of Arts Summer Show, 1991-6.
Architecture Tomorrow, AJ/Building Design Centre, 1996.
Greenwich Millennium Pavillions, RIBA Journal, The Architecture Foundation, 1996.
New British Architecture, The Architecture Foundation, 1994-5.
Under £50K, RIBA, London, 1993.

Further reading
RIBA Journal, Nov1996.
Architects' Journal, April + Sept 1996.
RIBA Journal, August 1996.
Building, August 1996.
Building Design, July 1996.

Anderson Christie Architects
382 Great Western Road
Glasgow G4 9HT
T: 0141 339 1515
F: 0141 339 0505

Resources
5 principal architects, 4 architectural technicians/assistants, 2 admin. staff.
CAD facilities and desktop publishing

Largest project value to date
£3.5 million, phase contracts totalling £5 million.

Professional indemnity
Yes.

Selected projects
Offices, Great Western Road, Glasgow.
£100,000, 1997.
Housing, Wellgate, Lanark. £260,000,1995.
Housing, Darnley, Glasgow. £3.2 million, 2 phases, 1997.
Housing, Glendore Street, Glasgow, £1.8 million, in progress 1997.

Awards/competitions
Erskine 2000, limited competition, residential care for the next Millennium, first place.
National Headquarters for Welfare State International, limited competition, second place.
Easterhouse Millennium Centre, Glasgow, open competition, second place.

Apicella Associates
Pentagram Design
11 Needham Road
London W11 2RP
T: 0171 229 3477
F: 0171 313 9608
E: email@pentagram.co.uk

Resources
2 associates, 1 architect, 5 architectural staff, 2 admin. staff.
8 Macintosh workstations, AutoCAD and MiniCAD, model-making skills.

Largest project value to date
£1.5 million.

Professional indemnity
Yes.

Selected projects
La Perla lingerie shop, London W1, £170,000, 1996-7.
R&D Headquarters, ADSHEL, London SW5, £1.5 million, 1997-8.
2nd floor Restaurant, Oxo Tower Wharf, London, £1 million, 1997.
Mobile merchandising and hospitality pavilions for Volvo UK, £600,000, 1997.
21st Century Theatre for WCT Live, 1997.

Awards/competitions
Aluminium Imagination Awards, highly commended 1993 and 1997.
Chartered Society of Designers Minerva Awards, highly commended 1993 and1994.
Design Week Awards, Interiors category 1991.
National Centre for Popular Music, Sheffield, 1996, shortlisted.
Royal Victoria Dock Footbridge, London, 1995, shortlisted.
Materials Gallery, 1995, shortlisted.
British Museum Reading Room, London, 1994, shortlisted.

Exhibitions
Portable Architecture, RIBA, 1997.
Royal Victoria Dock Footbridge competition, RIBA, 1995.
Windsor Castle competition entry, The Architecture Foundation, 1993.

Further reading
Building Design, 24 Oct 1997.
FX, October 1997.
Architects' Journal, 27 April 1994.
Architecture Today, Oct 1993.
Building Design, 18 May 1992.

B

Bareham Andrews Architects
Studio One
30-34 Aire Street
Leeds, LS1 4HT
T: 0113 245 7000

Resources
2 partners, 1 architect.
Microstation and MiniCAD.

Largest project value to date
£4.5 million.

Professional indemnity
Project insurance taken out where necessary.

Selected projects
Off-Centre Community Resource Centre, Leeds, 1996.
Visitor and Education Centre, Kirkstall Valley Nature Reserve, Leeds, £360,000, 1996.
Theatre + Arts Centre, Armagh, Northern Ireland, selected for exhibition, £3.8 million, 1996.
Northern Architecture Centre, £2 million,1997.

Awards/competitions
Northern Architecture Centre, 1997.
Concept House 1998.
The Hitman-Eddy family house, Brockhall, Lancashire, third prize winner, 1997.

Further reading
RIBA Journal, Sept 1997.
Building Design, Towards 2000 Nov 1995.
Architects' Journal, AJ 100, Feb 1995.

Beevor Mull Architects
The Studio
Wennington
Cambridgeshire PE17 2LX
T: 01487 773 259
F: 01487 773 304

Resources
3 architects, 1 general assistant and 1 consulting architect/town planner.

Largest project to date
£1.5 million.

Professional indemnity
Yes.

Selected projects
Maternity and Old People's Wing, Huntingdon, 1993-4.
Daycare centre with flats above for old people, 1996.
2 schemes of single person flats, 1992 and1997.
House for a wheelchair bound young woman and her parents,1995.
Sheltered housing scheme, Ramsey, 1995.
Self-built own house, 1995.
London home of newspaper proprietor, 1995.
2 community centres (one 50% lottery

funding), Hemingsford Abbots and Hartford, in progress 1997.
Foyer and civic intervention, Cambridge, in progress, 1997.

Awards/competitions
Foyer competition, The Architecture Foundation, 1992, shortlisted.

Exhibitions
Arts Council funded Quadratura project, architect/artist collaboration for an installation/exhibition, 1995.
Project with artist Edward Allington.
City of Bonn project for the IAAS, to be exhibited in Bonn.

Bere: Architects
24 Rosebery Avenue
London EC1R 4SX
T: 0171 837 9333
F: 0171 837 9444

Resources
6 full-time architectural staff, 2 part-time admin staff.
4 PCs on network: Microstation.
Fully equipped timber and metal workshop.

Largest project value to date
£1 million.

Professional indemnity
Yes.

Selected projects
Frameless glass facade, Next Retail, Oxford Street, London, 1997.
Twin bespoke, structural glass facades, Pizza Express, London Wall, London, 1996.
Car designer's mews house, Belsize Village, London, 1998.
Three new-build houses on backland mews site, Islington, London, 1998.
Private art gallery, Leicestershire, in progress 1997.
Rooftop addition to listed building, Mayfair, London, 1998.

Awards/competitions
RIBA Regional Award, shortlisted, Pizza Express, 1997.
Aluminium Imagination Award 1997, nominated.
Glassex Awards 1997, shortlisted.
RIBA Regional Award 1995, shortlisted.
Aluminium Imagination Award 1995, nominated.

Further reading
Building Design, May 30 1997.
Architectural Review, Feb 1997.
Architects' Journal (cover feature), Jan 16 1997.
Blueprint, October 1996.
World Architecture, June 1996.
Architectural Review, January 1996.
RIBA Journal, October 1995.

Birds Portchmouth Russum
8 New North Place
London EC2A 4JA
T: 0171 613 1777
F: 0171 613 2555
E: info@bprarchitects.co.uk

Resources
3 partners and 1 non-executive partner in New York, 2 architectural staff.
CAD workstations, model making.

Largest project value to date
£9 million.

Professional indemnity
Yes.

Selected projects
122-124 Haberdasher Street, refurbishment and extension of two existing flats, London, £100,000, 1986-7.
Avenue de Chartres Carpark, Chichester, £9 million, 1989-1991.
Croydon, Vision for The Future, Croydon, Feasibility study for the revitalisation of Croydon Town Centre, 1993.
A13 architectural and artistic proposals, architectural design for Canning Town to Beckton including design of new bridges, flyovers, underpasses, environmental barriers, lighting and modelling of Docklands tunnels entrance. £11.5 million, in progress 1997.
Culture-Dome, Fairfield Car-Park, Croydon. Feasibility study for design of exhibition and concert facilities on existing car park, £10 million, in progress 1997.

Awards/competitions
RIBA Regional Award 1992.
Civic Trust Award 1992.
West Sussex Council Design Award 1991.
English Tourist Board Car Park Design Award 1991.
The AJ Exterior Lighting Award 1992.
New Museum for Scottish Collection, Edinburgh, RIAS open competition for design of museum for the Scottish Collection, 1991.
Morecambe Sea Front, RIBA Competition, 1991.
Crossrail Station, Rickmansworth, England, £3 million, 1992.
Crystal Palace Park, 1996, Bromley Council, invited competition, second prize.
Imperial War Museum for the North, limited competition, 1997, second prize.

Exhibitions
Young British Architects Exhibition, The Architecture Foundation 1994.
Royal Academy Summer Exhibition, 1993.
Theory and Experimentation, Whiteleys, London, 1992.

Further reading
The Guardian, Jan 8, 1994.
The Guardian, June 6, 1994.
Building Design, May 22, 1992.
The Telegraph, Dec 31, 1994.

Boyarsky Murphy Architects
64 Oakley Square
London NW1 1NJ
T: 0171 388 3572
F: 0171 387 6776
E: mail@boyarskymurphy.com

Resources
2 principals, 1 architect, 1 architectural assistant, 1 admin.
Apple Macintosh workstations.

Largest project value to date
£250,000.

Professional indemnity
Yes.

Selected projects
Film House Media Centre, Paddington Basin, London, feasibility study, 1997.
McCloud Residence, London NW1, in progress.
Supreme Court, Nicosia, Cyprus, in progress.
2U greeting cards shop, London, conceptual design, 1996-7.
Ackermann residence, London W9, refurbishment and gallery design, 1996-7.

Awards/competitions
Europan housing competition for The Hague, 1996, prize-winners.

Further reading
Action Research, by Boyarsky and Murphy, (pub) Black Dog, London, 1997.
Architects' Journal, June 20 1996.
Techniques & Architecture, Aug/Sept 1996.
de Architect, Sept 1996.
Architects' Journal, October 1995.
Blueprint, May 1995.

Brady + Mallalieu
90 Queen's Drive
London N4 2HW
T: 0181 880 1544
F: 0181 880 2687

Resources
2 partners, 3 architects. 5 CAD workstations.

Largest project value to date
£3.5 million.

Professional indemnity
Yes.

Selected projects
University of North London, School of Architecture and Interior Design, Jan 1996, £2.25 million.
Irish Tourist Board Offices, London, January 1996, £250,000.
Groundwork, Hackney, London, 1995, £45,000.

Awards/competitions
RIBA Award, 1997, shortlisted.
RIAI Regional Award, 1995.

AAI Award, 1997.
Fingal County Hall competition, 1996, shortlisted.
Wakefield Grammar School, 1991, shortlisted.

Exhibitions
RAIA Regional Awards travelling exhibition, 1997, 1996, 1995, 1994.
30 under 50k, RIBA, 1992.
Progetthotel exhibition, Genoa, 1992.

Further reading
Building Design, May 23 1997.
Irish Architecture '97, March 1997.
RIBA Journal, Aug 1996.

Brookes Stacey Randall
34 Bruton Place
London W1X 7AA
T: 0171 495 2681
F: 0171 499 0733

Resources
4 partners, 1 architect, 9 architectural assistants, 2 admin.
12 Apple Macintosh workstations, Microstation, Form Z, Strata, Studio Pro.

Largest project value to date
£36 million.

Professional indemnity
Yes.

Selected projects
Wembley Park 2000 for London Underground, £1.5 million, phase 1 completed 1996.
Entschede bus and train station, Holland, redevelopment, 1995-6.
London Underground stations (Croxley Link), 1994.
Apartment for Chris Lowe of Pet Shop Boys, London, 1994.
The Thames Boathouse, Streatley, £98,000 1993.

Awards/competitions
RIBA Regional Award 1997.
Royal Fine Art Commission/Sunday Times Jeux d'Esprit Building of the Year Award 1995.
RIBA Regional Award 1995.
Glass and Glazing Award 1995.
Civic Trust Award 1995.
RIBA Regional Award, 1993.
Wembley Gateway competition, 1996.

Further reading
Building Envelope, by Alan Brookes, Architectural Press, 1996 (reprint).
Connections, by Alan Brookes, Architectural Press, 1996 (reprint).
Architects' Journal, January 11 1996.
Architecture Review, December 1993.

Bryant and Priest Architecture

Acorn House
43 Three Shires Oak Road
Bearwood, Warley
Birmingham B67 5DS
T: 0121 420 0040
F: 0121 429 1815

Resources
5 staff members,
Apple Macintoshes. 3D modelling.

Largest project value to date
£20 million.

Professional indemnity
Yes.

Selected projects
Cricket School at Edgbaston County Ground,
in collaboration with David Morley Architects,
£2.4 million, in progress 1997.
Loft project, Ludgate Hill, Birmingham,
£3 million, 1998.
The Drum, National Cultural Arts Centre,
Birmingham, £3.5 million, 1997.
Apollo Chemicals, Tamworth, Staffordshire,
£150,000, 1997.

Awards/competitions
Queensbridge School, Birmingham, new
perfomance spaces, competition, shortlisted,
1997.
Midlands Arts Centre redevelopment
competition, Cannon Hill Park, Birmingham,
second prize, 1997.

Further reading
Building Design, 3 October 1997.

Buschow Henley

21 Little Portland Street
London W1N 5AF
T: 0171 580 9800
F: 0171 580 9866
L: studio@bharch.demon.co.uk

Resources
5 architects, 6 architectural assistants
and 2 support staff.
Power Macintoshes, colour A1 plotting
facilities on the premises.

Largest project value to date
£4 million.

Professional Indemnity
Yes.

Selected projects
Michaelides and Bednash workplace, in
converted daylight factory, London W1,
£65,000, 1996.
Conversion of 1960s building for Prospect
Pictures, London W1, 1997.
Residential development conversion and new
build, Shepherdess Walk, London, £4million,
in progress 1997.

Childrens' Mobile Teaching Theatre, London,
£600,000 pending lottery funding bid, 1997.

Awards/competitions
Scottish Architecture and Design Centre
(SADC) competition,1995.
Sunlight Centre competition,1997.
D+AD Silver Award, 1997 and Design Council
Award, 1997 for Prospect Pictures offices.
D+AD Silver Award, 1997 (shortlisted), RAC
Exhibition Pavilion.
D+AD Silver Award, 1996 (shortlisted),
Michaelides and Bednash.

Exhibitions
RAC, UK Exhibition programme,
ongoing series.
Mazda, Pan-European Exhibition programme,
ongoing series.
'Aperture: A Camera Obscura' 'Ideal Rooms'
RIBA, London, 8 Sept-11 Oct, 1997.
'Architects and Exhibition Design 1900-1998',
RIBA Heinz Gallery, London, 22 Jan-14 March,
1998.

Further reading
New Office Design, by Francis Duffy &
Kenneth Powell, 1997, Conran Octopus.
D+AD Annual 1997.
Design Week, August 1997.
RIBA Journal, December 1996.
RIBA Journal, October 1996.
Blueprint, October 1996.
D+AD Annual 1996.
World Architecture, July1995.

Carter Reynolds

155 Upper Street
Islington
London N1 1RA
T: 0171 354 5403
F: 0171 354 5413
L: cr@carter-reynolds.demon.co.uk

Resources
4 staff expanding to 7.
Networked Power Macintosh workstations,
Internet.

Largest project value to date
£4.5 million.

Professional indemnity
Yes.

Selected projects
Private house refurbishment, Camden, London,
£90,000, 1985.
Private house annex, Battersea, London,
£30,000, 1995.
Rooftop extension, Hampstead, London,
£42,500, under construction, 1997.
Office building conversion, £800,000, 1997.
Doctors' surgery, Barking FHSA, new build,
£130,000, 1996.
Great Cornard Upper School masterplan,
scheme design, £4.5 million (lottery bid), 1997.

Awards/competitions
British Steel Melchett Award for innovative use
of stainless steel, 1993.
Central Middlesex Hospital NHS trust, Centre
for Women and Children competition, 1994,
commended.

Further reading
RIBA Journal, December 1996.

Caruso St John

12 Clerkenwell Road
London EC1M 5PI
T: 0171 251 6788
F: 0171 251 6799
E: caruso.stjohn@dial.pipex.com

Resources
5 architects, 2 architectural assistants
and 1 admin. staff.
Power Macintosh network, Microstation.

Largest project value to date
£15.75 million.

Professional Indemnity
Yes.

Selected projects
Walsall Art Gallery and Public Square,
£15.8million, completion due December
1998.
Highgate and Walsall Brewery, new public
house, Walsall, £540,000,1997.
2-6 Northburgh Street, office conversion,
London, £300,000, 1997.

Stratford Advice Arcade, East London,
£460,000, 1995.

Awards/competitions
Nara Convention Hall competition, Japan,
1990, special prize.
Yokahama International Terminal competition,
Japan, 1995, hon. mention.
Limmo Peninsula Ecocentre competition,
1995, finalist.

Exhibitions
Foyer Exhibition, The Architecture Foundation,
1992.
Between Patients, 10 Swan Yard, London N1,
1993.
New British Architecture, The Architecture
Foundation, 1994.
The Presence of Construction, Architectural
Association, Jan 1998.

Further reading
OASE 45/46 1997.
Arkitektur 3, April 1997.
Architects' Journal, January 18 1996.
Architecture + Detail, No.6 1996.
Building Design, August 9 1996.
Architecture and Urbanism11, No.314 1996.

Cottrell and Vermeulen Architecture
1a Iliffe Street,
London SE17 3QA
T: 0171 708 2567
F: 0171 252 4742

Resources
2 partners, 3 architectural staff.
2 PC intel computers with AutoCAD,
Photoshop, scanner, A2 colour printer.

Largest project value to date
£900,000 (phased).

Professional Indemnity
Yes.

Selected projects
St Martin's Church, London E13, refurbishment
and new community building, £500,000,
1996-7, lottery funding received.
House extension, Leigh-on-Sea, £75,000,
1993-6.
Westborough Primary School, Westcliff-on-
Sea, refurbishment (1993-5), 4 new
classrooms (1996), new nursery/playground
structure (1997) £900,000.
Milton Hall Primary School, Westcliff-on-Sea,
8 new classrooms and refurbishment (1995-
6), new nursery (1996), £600,000.

Exhibitions
RIBA Heinz Gallery, London, 'Colour &
Architecture', 1992.
RIBA, London, 'First Sight', March/April 1995.

Further reading
Architects' Journal, January 9 1997.
Building Design, January 31 1997.
Architects' Journal, February 20 1997.
RIBA Journal, August 1997.

D

David Mikhail Architects
68-74 Rochester Place
London NW1 9JX
T: 0171 485 4696
F: 0171 267 8661

Resources
1 principal architect, 2 architectural assistants
(part time), business manager (part time).
2 computers.

Largest project value to date
£1 million.

Professional indemnity
Yes.

Selected projects
London Print Workshop new-build gallery,
offices and workshop, London W10, £1 million
(lottery bid), completion July 1998.
Speculative private house, Uxbridge Street,
London, £600,000, completion 1998.
House and offices, St Helier, Jersey,
£250,000, completion December 1998.
Speculative private house, London W11,
£180,000 , 1997.
Soho Fashion Showroom, London WC1,
£30,000, 1994.

Awards/competitions
Foyer competition, Architecture
Foundation,1993, shortlisted.
RIBA competition, Snowdonia Business Park,
1992, runner up.
Europan 2, Zagreb site, 1991, winner.

Exhibitions
Open House, public access to new-build
house, London W11, 1997.
Under £40,000 exhibition, RIBA and Ruth
Aram, Hampstead, 1994.
Foyer exhibition, Architecture Foundation,
1993.

Further reading
Architecture Today, September 1997.
Blueprint, March 1997.
RIBA Journal, February 1996.
Building Design, June 16 1995.

David Sheppard Architect
Tan Cottage
49 Fore Street
Plympton St Maurice
Plymouth PL7 3LZ
T: 01752 336 333

Resources
1 principal architect, 1 architect,
1 part-time CAD technician/architect,
1 part-time secretary.
2 CAD workstations. 2D, 3D models and video
walk-throughs. Model-making facility, Internet.

Largest project value to date
£2.5 million.

Professional indemnity
Yes.

Selected projects
Lonkiewicz Library and Repository, £2.5 million, completion 1996.
Environmentally-conscious Industrial Unit, Poole, Dorset, £500,000, detailed planning Oct 1997.
New house, Casablanca, Morocco, £1.2 million, completion 1999.
New house with rammed earth walls, Westlake Brake, Devon, £135,000, 1997.
Cedar House, Salisbury, £110,000, 1996.

Awards/competitions
RIBA Regional Awards 1997, shortlisted for The Cedar House, Salisbury.

Further reading
West Country television documentary on the Westlake Brake House, transmission September 1997.

de Rijke Marsh Morgan
Clink Street Studios
1 Clink Street
London SE1 9DG
T: 0171 407 1117
F: 0171 407 1118

Resources
3 partners, 7 architectural staff
4 Macintosh workstations, MiniCAD, Photoshop, QuarkXpress, Illustrator.

Largest project value to date
£750,000.

Professional indemnity
Project by project basis.

Selected projects
Urban proposals for Plymouth City Centre, 1996–7
New housing complex in Holland,1996–7
Chain of 5 fitness centres, converting basement car parks, central London, £750,000, 1996–7.
Folly conversion into tower dwelling, Derbyshire, 1996-7.
Remodelling of family house, Queen's Park, London, 1996-7.
Covered exercise pool for country club, Kent, 1996-7.
Ecostation, Limmo peninsular, London Docklands, competition winner, £700,000, 1995–6

Awards/competitions
British Crafts Council exhibition design, 1997.
Plymouth City Centre urban planning competition(with PACA), 1996, winner.
Conversion of listed 18th century farm building, Limmo ecostation competition, winner, 1994.
Devon, RIBA Regional Award, 1993.
Summer Street competition, 1992, winner.
British Steel TramStop competition (with David Adjaye), 1992, 2nd prize.

Exhibitions
Royal Academy Summer Exhibition, 1996.
Architects' Journal centenary exhibition, London, 1995.
New British Architecture, The Architecture Foundation,1994.
Summer Street Competition, London, 1993.

Further reading
Blueprint, Jan + Dec 1995.

E & F McLachlan Architects
North Bridge House
28 North Bridge
Edinburgh EH1 1QG
T: 0131 990 1350
F: 0131 990 5100

Resources
2 partners, 1 architectural assistant.
3 Apple Macintosh workstations,
3D CAD Modelshop.

Largest project value to date
£1.1 million.

Professional indemnity
Yes.

Selected projects
Holyrood North, Edinburgh, 16 flats, £768,000, on site 1998.
South Gyle, Edinburgh, 27 apartments/houses, £1.1million, opened spring 1997.
Matthew Architecture Gallery, Edinburgh, 1992.

Awards/competitions
South Gyle housing, Saltire, Awards for Design Excellence, 1997.
Holyrood North, Edinburgh, conversion of brewery copper house into offices, limited competition, 1996 winner.
Colour in the Built Environment, Crown Berger award1992.

Further reading
Forty under 40, RIBA catalogue, 1988.
RIBA Journal, Dec 1996.
RIBA Journal, Feb 1997.

East
10, Crossley Street
London N7 8PD
T/F: 0171 607 4736

Resources
2 principals, 2 staff.
Apple Macintosh system, Microstation

Largest project value to date
£900,000.

Professional indemnity
Yes.

Selected projects
Stratford Advice Arcade, London, refurbished 1950s office, £470,000, 1995.
Oxleas Interpretation Centre proposal, £250,000, 1996.
Brader Perryman Offices, West London, £25,000, 1995.
Borough High Street, London, part of £1m environmental improvements, The Architecture Foundation's Future Southwark design initiative,1997.

F

Awards/competitions
Europan 3 Competition, Marl site, winning entry, 1994.
Priesthill housing competition.
Glasgow, Europan 4,1996.
Sittingbourne Settlement Competition, second placed prize, with Sergison Bates Architects, 1997.

Further reading
Architecture Today, September 1995.
Building Design, June 7,1996.
Rivers of Meaning, London Rivers Association, 1996.
Cambridge Architecture Journal, Issue 9, 1997.

Ellis-Miller Architects & Designers
8 Pound Hill
Cambridge CB3 0AE
T: 01223 359000
F: 01223 359900

Resources
2 architects, 1 architectural staff.

Largest project value to date
£2.5 million.

Professional indemnity
Yes.

Selected projects
Swimming pool and gymnasium facilities, 1997.
Restoration of Ufford Hall, 1997.
New Cricket Pavilion for Prickwillow CC, 1997.
David Hockney Exhibition Design, Cambridge Arts,1997.
New house and studio for Mary Reyner Banham, 1996.
Medway Tunnel East and West service buildings, £2.5million, 1994.

Awards/competitions
Galvanizing Association Award, 1997.
RIBA Award, 1993, House at Prickwillow Thames Bridge Competition, 1993, commendation.
RIBA Regional Award, 1991.

Exhibitions
Home Exhibition, Gallery 2 RIBA, 1996.
Modern Steel House Exhibition, RIBA, 1996.
Greenwich Millennium Pavillions, RIBA Journal The Architecture Foundation, 1996.

FAT
12 – 16 Clerkenwell Road
London EC1M 5PL
T: 0171 251 6735
F: 0171 251 6738
E: fat@fat.co.uk
www.fat.co.uk

Resources
5 principals, 5 other architectural staff as needed. Graphic design and model-making facilities.
Power Mac workstations, computer rendering and Photoshop.

Largest project to date
£1.2 million.

Professional indemnity
Projects are indemnified individually.

Selected projects
The Scala, cinema conversion, King's Cross, London, £1.2 million, 1997.
House conversion for comedian Steve Coogan, London,1997.
ICA, redesign of bar, café, lower galleries, London,1997.
Advertising Agency, Amsterdam, conversion of church into office, 1997.
The Chez Garson, conversion of chapel into a house, London,1996.
The Brunel Rooms, leisure development, Swindon, £500,000, 1995.

Exhibitions
Cities on the Edge exhibition design, RIBA, 1997.
Roadworks, audio-visual art installations, 10 bus shelters in central London, 1996.
Architecture on the Horizon, RIBA, 1996.

Further reading
Experience, (pub) Booth Clibborn Editions, 1995.
Theory and Experimentation, (pub) Academy Editions, 1992.
Blueprint, April 1997.
Design Week, March 21, 1997.
Blueprint, December 1996.
Architects' Journal, November 7, 1996.

Foreign Office Architects Ltd
58 Belgrave Road
London SW1V 2BP
T: 0171 976 5988
F: 0171 630 9754
E: foa@easynet.co.uk

Resources
2 principals, 3 staff.
CAD facilities.

Largest project value to date
£150 million.

Professional indemnity
Projects are indemnified individually.

Selected projects
Bermondsey Antiques Market, design commission, Southwark, London1997.
Mirage City, urban design ideas study, Tokyo,1997.
Yokohama International Ferry Terminal, £150 million, design development in progress 1996-7.
Private house, Sussex, 1995.
Cambridge Lodge, extension of a residence for the elderly, Sussex, 1992

Awards/competitions
Virtual House invited competition, Any Corporation, USA,1997.
Meyong-Dong Cathedral of Seoul, Korea, 1995-6, 2nd prize winner.
Yokohama International Ferry Terminal competition,1995, winner.

Exhibitions
New Landscapes exhibition, Museum of Contemporary Arts Barcelona, Spain, 1997.
Virtual Architecture exhibition, Tokyo University gallery,1997.
Architecture on the Horizon exhibition, Academy Group /RIBA Architecture Centre, London,1996.

Further reading
Building Design, June 20 1997.
GA Japan, January 1997.
Building Design, October 11 1996.
Architectural Design August 1996.
AA Files. Summer 1995.
Arch+ September1995.

Gollifer Associates

Second floor
1-2 Great Chapel Street
London W1V 3AG
T: 0171 734 2134
F: 0171 494 99 17

Resources
4–6 architectural staff, 1 admin.
4 Macintosh Power PC workstations, MiniCAD,
Microstation, Form Z, A1 plotting facility,
desktop publishing.
Model-making facilities.

Largest project value to date
£7.2 million.

Professional indemnity
Yes.

Selected projects
National Glass Centre, Sunderland,
£7.2 million (approx £5million lottery funded),
completion1998.
Ally Capellino shop, London SW3, £175,000,
1997.
Soho 601, post production facility, Dean Street,
London, £1.2 million, 1996.
Atelier Restaurant, Beak Street, London,
£50,000, 1994.

Awards/competitions
Design Week Awards, 1994, shortlisted.
National Glass Centre competition, winner
1994.

Harper Mackay

33 – 37 Charterhouse Square
London EC1M 6EA
T: 0171 600 5151
F: 0171 600 1092
E: design@harper-mackay.co.uk

Resources
2 senior directors, 2 partners, 25 architects,
7 architectural staff.
MiniCAD/DTP/Quicktime animation.

Largest project value to date
£800 million.

Professional indemnity
Yes.

Selected projects
M&C Saatchi, headquarters refurbishment,
London, £5.1 million, 1997.
Derwent Valley Holdings, part refurbishment
and new build of offices, London, £5.1 million,
1998.
Polygram UK, fitout of offices, London, £1.2
million, 1997.
British Petroleum, design for permanent
exhibition, £1.1 million, 1996.
Ian Schrager Hotels, two conversions of offices
to hotels, London, first stage 1999.

Awards/competitions
Office of the Year, British Institute of Facilities
Managers, small office first prize 1996.
Design Week Awards, shortlisted 1995.
Highlight Award, 1995.
Design Week Awards, 1994.
National Association of Shopfitters Award,
1994.

Further reading
Architects' Journal, Sept 25 1997.

Harrison Ince

2 Jordan Street
Knott Mill
Manchester
M15 4PY
T: 0161 236 3650
F: 0161 236 9997
E: cad@harrison-ince.co.uk

Resources
2 partners, 2 architects, 2 architectural
technicians, 1 interior designer and 2 admin.
Expanding network of computer workstations:
AutoCAD Release 13, AEC and AccuRender
(3-D), in house model makers and colour
plotting facilities.

Largest project value to date
£4.5m. Feasibility projects up to £0m.

Professional indemnity
Yes.

Selected projects
Furzton Lake bar/restaurant and hotel, Milton

Keynes, £3.5million, 1995-7.
Mash and Air bar/restaurant, Manchester,
£2.1million, 1996.
Barca bar/restaurant, Manchester, £700,000,
1995-6.
Communique Offices, Manchester, £250,000,
1996.

Awards/competitions
Manchester Society of Architects Design
Award (unbuilt projects) 1995.
Manchester Society of Architects Design
Award (building in the city) 1997.
RIBA Regional Awards, shortlisted 1997.
CNT Design Award, 1996.
Martinscroft, lodge and restaurant, Warrington,
competition, 1992, winner.

Further reading
Theme Magazine, January 1997.
Theme Magazine, June 1997.
Theme Magazine, June 1996.
Architects' Journal, April 3,1997.
Building, April 1997.
Arena Magazine, March 1997.
Design Week, August 8,1997.

Hawkins Brown
60 Bastwick Street
London EC1V 3PN
T: 0171 336 8030
F: 0171 336 8851

Resources
2 partners, 10 architects, 3 architectural
assistants, 5 technical staff. CAD facilities.

Largest project value to date
£19.5 million.

Professional indemnity
Yes.

Selected projects
The Donnington Collection, Formula One
Museum, £13 million (lottery bid), due 1999.
Brunswick Centre, Camden, retail mall
refurbishment, London, £1.75 million, due
1998.
Hackney Community College, refurbishment,
London, £2.6 million, 1997.
Faculty of Arts, Southampton University,
refurbishment, £6.2 million, 1996.
The Henry Moore Foundation, library extension,
Perry Green, £400,000, 1994.

Awards/competitions
RIBA/Times Community Funding Award, 1997.
Birmingham Design Initiative Awards, 1997,
commendation.
RIBA Architecture Awards 1997, 2 projects
shortlisted).
Civic Trust Awards 1997, shortlisted.
RIBA Eastern Region Award 1996, shortlisted.

Further reading
RIBA Journal, January 1997.
RIBA Journal, August 1997.

Architects' Journal, May 29, 1997.
Blueprint, July 1997.

Hodder Associates
Commercial Wharf
6 Commercial Street
Manchester M15 4PZ
T: 0161 834 6002
F: 0161 839 8940

Resources
1 senior partner, 2 associate partners,
8 architects, 4 architectural staff,
2 technical staff.
Apple Macintosh and PC workstations,
Microstation, Photoshop, QuarkXpress,
Stratavision.

Largest project value to date
£17 million.

Professional indemnity
Yes.

Selected projects
New Golf Club House, High Leigh, £800,000
on site 1997.
Gallery of Contemporary Architecture and
Design, Manchester, £250,000, in progress
1997.
City Road Surgery, Manchester, £235,000,
1996.
Centenary Building, University of Salford,
1996.
St Catherine's College extension, Oxford,1995.
New Swimming Pool, Colne, £1.5million, 1992.

Awards/competitions
The Stirling Prize 1996 for Centenary Building,
University of Salford.
RIBA Award 1996.
RIBA Architecture in Education category
Award, 1996.
RIBA Award 1996 for City Road Surgery,
Hulme.
RA Summer Exhibition 1995, Grand Prize for
Manchester City Art Gallery.
RIBA Award 1994, Oswald Medical Centre.

Further reading
International Architecture Year Book 1997.
RIBA Journal, July 1996.
RIBA Journal, Feb 1995.

Hudson Featherstone
49 – 59 Old Street
London EC1V 9HX
T: 0171 490 5656
F: 071 490 5757

Resources
5 architectural staff, 1 admin.
Apple Mac CAD system.

Largest project value to date
£700,000.

Professional indemnity
Yes.

Selected projects
Tilt House, grass-roofed courtyard house,
north Cornwall, £250,000, in progress 1997.
William Tyndale School, extension, in progress
1997.
The Bean, coffee bar, Shoreditch, £10,000,
1996 (in collaboration with Andrew Waugh).
Quarto Publishing House, new offices,
£350,000, 1996.

Awards/competitions
Civic Trust Award, 1997, Baggy House.
Sunday Times/ Royal Fine Art Commission
Building of the Year 1995, Baggy House.
Time Out Nightclub of the Year, 1995,
The Blue Note.

Exhibitions
How Did They Do That? The Building of Baggy
House, 1995, RIBA, London.
Loft2, 1995, Florence Gallery, RIBA.
First Sight, 1995, RIBA.
Exhibitor at the Royal Academy Summer
Exhibition, 1987.

Further reading
The Sunday Times, Sept 71997.
Building Design, May 9, 1997.
Marie Claire Maison, February 1997.
Building Homes, November 1996.
Elle Decoration, July 1996.

Hugh Broughton Architects
4 Addison Bridge Place
London W14 8XP
T: 0171 602 8840
F: 0171 602 5254

Resources
3 architects (dependent on workload).
Apple Macintosh workstations, MiniCAD,
Microstation, PowerDraw and Photoshop.

Largest project value to date
£2 million.

Professional indemnity
Yes.

Selected projects
Congress House, refurbishment, London,
£1.8 million,1997.
Guide Association building, Wimbledon,
London, £160,000, in progress1997.
RSA Great Room restoration, London,
£650,000,1996.
Apartment, Holland Park, London,
£70,000,1996.

Further reading
Building Design, February 7 1997.
Architects's Journal, May 29 1997.
RIBA Journal, Sept 1997.
Essential Kitchens, Sept 1997.
Diseño Interior, Autumn 1997.

Ian Simpson Architects
Commercial Wharf
6 Commercial Street
Manchester M15 4PZ
T: 0101 839 4804
F: 0161 839 4808

26 Britton Street
London EC1 5NQ
T: 0171 251 8784
F: 0171 490 5331

Resources
Total 20 staff in two offices, all CAD-trained.
3 directors/architects, 7 architects, 7 other
architectural staff and 3 technical staff.
CAD, 3D modelling and visualisation
techniques.

Largest project value to date
£8.8 million.

Professional indemnity
Yes.

Selected projects
Manchester Museum, Manchester University,
(awarded £8.8 million lottery funding) 1997.
Foyer, Birmingham, £2.25 million, due for
completion 1998.
Merchants Warehouse restoration, Manchester,
£2.6 million, 1996.
Atlas Bar Cafe, Manchester, 1994.

Awards/competitions
Rebuilding Manchester, £500 million urban
design competition, with EDAW, Baxter, Benoy,
first prize.
Landscape proposals for a new park, Hulme,
competition, first prize.
Foyer competition, The Architecture
Foundation, first prize.

Further reading
RIBA Journal, February 1997.
RIBA Interiors, September 1996.
RIBA Journal, August 1996.
Building Design, April 26, 1996.
RIBA Journal, November 1995.

John Brennan Architect
1 Crown Street
Edinburgh EH0 8LU
T: 0131 903 3119
E: jba@blinternet.com

Resources
Sole practitioner, supplemented as needed.
Apple Macintosh CAD facilities, Photoshop,
Videoshop, dtp.

Largest project value to date
£320,000.

Professional indemnity
Yes.

Selected projects
Highland Eco House, Ullapool, (joint project),
£250,000, due for completion 1998.
New Lives, New Landscapes Ltd, feasibility
study due for completion 1998.
Lowland Croft, West Lothian, £120,000,
due for completion 1998.
Farmhouse, Comrie, Perthshire, £300,000,
due for completion 1998.

Awards/competitions
BT WWF Partnership Award, environment in
the community, 1996.

Further reading
Eco-Sustainable Architecture, Construction
and Design, Eco, June 1997.
Resurgence Magazine, April 1995.

John Pardey Architect
The Studio
Eastwood
Ridgeway Lane
Lymington
Hampshire SO41 8AA
T: 01590 677 226

Resources
Sole practitioner, CAD facilities.

Largest project value to date
£5.5 million.

Professional indemnity
Project by project basis.

Selected projects
Crematorium, £1.5 million, awaiting funding
1997.
House, Lymington, £143,000, 1993.
House, New Forest, £100,000, 1994.

Awards/competitions
RIBA /Centro Bus Station, Walsall,
competition, 1995, commendation.
Europan 2 competition, 1996, Priesthill site,
runner-up.

Further reading
Build It, September 1997.
Architects' Journal, December 8, 1993.

K

Knott Architects

11b Rosemary Works
Branch Place
London N1 5PH
T+ F: 0171 729 8558

Resources
2 partners, additional team members as needed.
Word processing workstations; CAD imminent.

Largest project to date
£500,000.

Professional indemnity
Yes.

Selected projects
Glazed reception, Haymarket Publishing, Teddington, in progress1997.
2-level loft apartment fit-out, Bankside, London, in progress1997.
Big Breakfast Show studio reconstruction, London, 1996.
Loft apartment fit-out, Wardour Street, London, 1996.
Weaving studio roof extension, Oxford, 1994.
Conversion of millinery works to antique/exhibition galleries and apartments, London, 1996.

Awards/competitions
Sunlight Centre competition, community centre, Gillingham, 1997, commended.
People's Palace competition, Building Design, 1994, highly commended.

Further reading
Architects' Journal, September 9, 1997.
Architects' Journal, May 9, 1997.
Architects' Journal, January 16, 1997.
Building Design, June 13, 1997.
Times Magazine, June 7, 1996.

L

Lee Boyd Partnership

6 Canaan Lane
Edinburgh EH10 4SY
T: 0131 447 1818
F: 0131 447 8799
E: design@leeboyd.co.uk

Resources
8 architects, 3 assistants, 1 CAD manager, 2 admin. staff.
8 Apple Macintosh CAD workstations, 3 PC CAD workstations, 2 Apple Macintosh admin. workstations. ArchiCAD (3d), AutoCAD and PowerCAD, Freehand, Photoshop and Pagemaker.

Largest project value to date
£12 million.

Professional indemnity
Yes.

Selected projects
National Library of Scotland, refurbishment, £10 million, 1997.
New Museum of Scotland exhibition, £2.5 million, lottery-funded, 1997.
Edinburgh Park office building, £2.5 million, 1997.
Edinburgh Royal Infirmary, masterplan, collaboration,1994.

Awards/competitions
Regeneration Design Awards,1994, commended.
RIBA Award 1996, shortlisted.
Galvanising Award, 1996, commendation.
Architects' Journal Small Projects Award, 1996, 2 projects commended.

Further reading
Museums in Britain Magazine, Spring 1997
Scotsman Weekend Supplement, July 27, 1996.
Museums in Britain Magazine, Spring 1996.
Museums in Britain Magazine, Summer 1996.
RIAS Prospect Magazine, Spring 1996.
RIAS Prospect Magazine, Autumn 1989.
Fire Protection Magazine, May 1992.

Loader and Brown Architects

A3 4th Floor
Linton House
39 – 51 Highgate Road
London NW5 1RT
T: 0171 267 0636
F: 0171 267 6911

Resources
2 architects, 1 architectural staff, assistants employed as necessary.
2 computers, Microstation and MiniCAD.

Largest project value to date
Feasibility studies /masterplanning £36 million, building projects £500,000.

Professional indemnity
Yes.

Selected projects
Nursery for Chameleon Management, London, £130,000, 1997.
Refugee Support Centre, Salusbury School, London, £45,000 lottery funding, in progress 1997.
Capital Challenge bid, Gospel Oak, London, £6 million, in progress 1997.
Housing proposal for 61 apartments, Gävle, Sweden, £5 million, in planning 1997.

Awards/competitions
Europan 3 competition, 1993, Gävle, Sweden, site, winner.
Upper Heyford US Airforce base conversion masterplan competition 1996, commended.

Maccreanor + Lavington Architects
A2 4th Floor
Linton House
39-51 Highgate Road
London NW5 1RT
T: 0171 482 5222
F: 0171 267 2836

Pelgrimsstraat 5
3029 BH Rotterdam
Netherlands
T: 31(0)10 478 2292
F: 31(0)10 276 2112

Resources
Each office has 1 partner, 3 staff, 3 Apple Macintosh computers CAD and 3D facilities.

Largest project value to date
£2.45 million (UK), £10 million (Netherlands).

Professional indemnity
Yes.

Selected projects
Housing, Zaaneiland, Netherlands, £10 million, 1993-6.
Lux Centre for film, video and new media, Hoxton Square, London, lottery funded, shell and core £1.75 million, fitout £650,000, 1997.
Apartment buildings, Ypenburg, Netherlands, urban expansion, £2.6 million, in progress 1997.

Awards/competitions
Prix de Rome, Netherlands Architectural Award, 1995, commended.
Bergen op Zoom Hotel competition, 1993, first prize.
Europan II, Zaanstad housing competition, 1992, first prize.

Exhibitions
New British Architecture, The Architecture Foundation, 1994.
Europan, Netherlands Architecture Institute, 1993.
40 under £60K, RIBA, London, 1994.

Further reading
A+T magazine (Madrid), December 1996.
RIBA Journal, November 1996.
RIBA Journal, October 1995.

Malcolm Fraser Architects
28 North Bridge
Edinburgh EH1 1QG
T: 0131 225 2585
F: 0131 220 1895

Resources
1 principal, 5 project architects, 1 interior designer, 6 architectural assistants and 1 office admin.
CAD facilities.

Largest project value to date
£4.25 million.

Professional indemnity
Yes.

Selected projects
Scottish Poetry Library, Canongate, Edinburgh, £900,000 (lottery funded), on site, 1997.
Dance Base regional dance centre, Grassmarket, Edinburgh, £4 million (lottery bid), 1997.
Pizza Express chain, 8 sites in Scotland, 2 complete in 1997, 2 on site, £300-500,000 each.
Buchanan's Court, offices and other facilities, Edinburgh, £1.2 million, 1992.

Awards/competitions
Royal Scottish Academy Gold Medal for Scottish Poetry Library, 1997.

Further reading
RIBA Journal, October 1997.

Mark Fisher Architects
26 Edbrooke Road
London W9 2DG
T: 0171 266 4445
F: 0171 286 7202

Resources
2 architects.
3 Apple Macintosh workstations, MiniCAD.

Largest project value to date
£4 million.

Professional indemnity
Yes.

Selected projects
Innovation and Technology Transfer Centre, Plymouth, £3.2 million, 1995.
Retail outlet series for Warehouse Group, Newcastle.
Office building, Walsall, 1996, RAC invited competition winner, £3.5 million.
Modular small station prototype feasibility for Railtrack Property, rolling programme 1997.

Awards/competitions
Concept House, Workplace 98 Exhibition, 2nd prize.
Temple Bridge Housing, AJ Inhabited Bridge competition, 1996.

Matthew Lloyd Architects
First Floor, 39-41 Folgate Street
London E1 6DX
T: 0171 377 1096
F: 0171 247 4317
E: matthewlloyd@dial.pipex.com

Resources
3 registered architects, 2 architectural assistants, 1 architectural technician, 1 office manager.
4 Power Macintoshes (networked), MiniCAD, Photoshop.

Largest project value to date
£1.5million.

Professional indemnity
Yes.

Selected projects
Harrow Club and Vicarage, youth and community centre, London, refurbishment, £1.5million, (lottery funded) on site1998.
Move-On housing over shops, Brick Lane, London, £700,000, on site1997.
New family house in conservation area, London E1, £225,000, 1997.
New flats and shops, Portobello Road, London, £190,000, 1997.

Awards/competitions
Hackney Empire Theatre refurbishment competition, London,1997, shortlisted.
Limmo Peninsular Ecology Interpretative Centre, London Docklands, 1995, shortlisted.
Gateways to Burgess Park, Southwark competition, London,1994, first prize.

Exhibitions
New British Architecture, The Architecture Foundation, 1994.

Further Reading
RIBA Journal, April 1994.
Blueprint, April 1994.

Matthew Priestman Architects
6-8 Emerald Street
London WC1N 3QA
T: 0171 404 3113
F: 0171 404 1661
E: mpa@mparch.demon.co.uk

Resources
2 partners, 2 architects, 2 assistants.
CAD facilities.

Largest project value to date
£1.3 million.

Professional indemnity
Yes.

Selected projects
University College of South Stockholm, 350,000 sq.m masterplan for teaching and research facilities, in development, 1997.
Cheshire Home, Hertfordshire, redevelopment of disabled persons residential home, in progress 1997.
Orestaden New Town, Denmark, masterplan for 34 million sq. ft. mixed use extension to Copenhagen, unbuilt.
Kingswell Centre, London, retail and residential conversion, £1.3 million, 1996.
19 and 20 Pembridge Mews, London, two mews conversions, £40,000 and £60,000, 1993.
House, Calbourne Road, London, 1992.
Fitzjohns Avenue, London, conversion of flat and roof addition, £50,000,1990.

Awards/competitions
University College of South Stockholm, international competition winner, 1996.
Orestaden competition, Denmark, 1994, first prize.
AJ Bovis Award,1992 Kuwait International Health Club.
Bangour Hospital Development, Edinburgh, competition 1994, first prize.
Cheshire Home, Hertfordshire, competition 1992, winner.

McDowell + Benedetti
62 Rosebery Avenue
London EC1R 4RR
T: 0171 278 8810
F: 0171 278 8844

Resources
2 partners, 5 other architectural staff, 1 technical staff.
3 Apple Macintosh workstations, MiniCAD.

Largest project to date
£450,000, $1 billion in collaboration with YRM.

Professional indemnity
Yes.

Selected projects
DNA art gallery, London, lottery bid, in progress 1997.
Oliver's Wharf penthouse refurbishment, £450,000,1997.
Fashion company HQ refurbishment, King's Cross, London, £350,000,1997.
Jigsaw Menswear Shop, Mayfair, London, £350,000, 1997.
100-apartment, 10-storey building on the Thames in Docklands, London, £10 million, planning application, 1997.
Tubs Hill House, Sevenoaks, Kent, £250,000,1994.

Awards/competitions
Millennium Bridge competition, RIBA/Financial Times,1997, shortlisted.
RAIA Smithfield regeneration international competition, Dublin 1991, winner.
RIBA Downland Award, 1994, shortlisted.

Further reading
Architects' Journal, August 7, 1997
Architects' Journal, January 5, 1994.
Sunday Times, June 8, 1997.
Sunday Times, February 9, 1997.
Evening Standard, July 23 1997.
Evening Standard, June 11 1997.

A. McInnes Gardner & Partners
7 Lynedoch Crescent
Glasgow G3 6DZ
T: 0141 332 3815
F: 0141 332 5295
E: info@mcinnesgardner.co.uk

Resources
2 partners, 11 staff.
CAD facilities, visualisations, animations and interactive CD multimedia facilities.

Largest project value to date.
£25 million.

Professional indemnity
Yes.

Selected projects
Holiday house, Kyle of Bute, £450,000, 1997.
New assembly plant, re-modelled admin block and elevation, Kirkintilloch, £1.2million, 1995.
New plastic moulding workshop, Kirkintilloch, £1.6million, in progress 1997.
Ticket centre, Candleriggs, Glasgow, 1995.

Awards/competitions
Glasgow Institute of Architects Design Award, 1997.
Urban Regeneration Design Award,1996.
RIAS Urban Regeneration Design Award 1995.

MUF Architects
49–51 Central Street
London EC1V 8AB
T: 0171 251 4004
F: 0171 250 1967

Resources
Total 9 staff: 5 architects, 2 artists, 2 technical staff.
Fully networked PowerMac system (including scanner and printing facilities), AutoCAD, Microstation, MiniCAD and Photoshop.

Largest project value to date
Competitions up to £10m. Largest project to date £1.2 million.

Professional indemnity
Yes.

Selected projects
Millennium Dome, London, selected to work on development of the environment of the dome, in progress 1997.
Southwark Street, London, urban regeneration, The Architecture Foundation's Future Southwark design initiative £1.2 million, in progress 1997.
Hackney Walkways and Digital Cultural Map project, London, 1997, £130,000.
Lasdun Retrospective exhibition, Royal Academy of Arts, London,1997, £30,000.
21st Century Living and Eco Transport Exhibition, Earth Centre, Doncaster, 1997, £300,000.

Exhibition Design for Helen Storey, ICA London, 1997, £10,000.
Loft, London, 1996, £30,000.

Awards/competitions
London Arts Board, 1997, research grant for Multiple Histories.
Arts Council Architecture Unit, 1996, research grant for Shared Ground.
RSA, Art and Architecture Awards, 1996, funding for 3 Films.
Arts Council Architecture Unit, 1994, feasibility study grants.

Exhibitions
Public Views, The Architecture Foundation, 1995.

Further reading
Building Design, February14, 1997.
Building Design, Feb. 7, 1997.
Building Design, April17, 1997.
The Observer, February 9, 1997.
Mama, February 1997.
Archis, September 1996.
Scroope, September 1996.
AD, August 1996.
Building Design, February 2, 1996.
Building Design, June 7, 1996.
Building Design, December 6, 1996.

Niall McLaughlin Architects

166 Portobello Road
London W11 2EB
T: 0171 792 0973
F: 0171 243 4081
E: mmclaughlin@compuserve.com

Resources
Staff increases to 3 dependent on workload.

Largest project value to date
£500,000. Projects up to £1m are anticipated.

Professional indemnity
Yes.

Selected projects
House, Knightsbridge, London, £400,000, 1996.
Hide for a photographer, Northants, £15,000, 1995.
Monastery, Kensington, London, £800,000, 1993.
Swimming pool, Kensington, London, £400,000, 1995.
Apartment, Notting Hill Gate, London, £100,000, 1992.

Awards/competitions
RAIA regional award, swimming pool, 1997.
Daily Telegraph Contemporary House of the Year 1997.
RAIA regional award for monastery 1996.

Exhibitions
British Architecture: New Work Future Visions, touring exhibition, 1997.

OMI Architects

King Street Buildings
1 Ridgefield
Manchester M2 6EG
T: 0161 832 3242
F: 0161 832 9929
E: omi@good.co.uk

Resources
5 architects (2 equal directors, 2 associate directors and 1 year-out student), 1 secretary. 3 Apple Mac workstations; Form Z and 3-D modelling.

Largest project value to date
£8 million.

Professional indemnity
Yes.

Selected projects
Hulme redevelopment, Manchester, mixed use housing scheme, £7.5 million, 1996.
Pump House Museum, Manchester, conversion of listed Edwardian pumping station into new museum, £1million, 1994.
Boarshurst Farm, Oldham, group of new and converted dwellings, £1million, 1991.
Albert Hall, Manchester, manipulation of listed meeting hall to create a 12-storey office development, £9 million, listed building consent obtained 1993.

Awards/competitions
Civic Trust Commendations, The Pump House, People's History Museum and Boarshurst Farm Housing Development,1995.
Gulbenkian Award, City Art Gallery Café, Manchester 1991.
RIBA Housing Awards, Boarshurst Farm and Boundary Lane 1995.
RIBA Housing awards, Hulme and Bonsall Street 1996.
MSA Awards for Boundary Lane, Hulme and Bonsall Street, Hulme, 1996.

Further reading
Architects' Journal, August 14 1991.
Architects' Journal, April 20,1994.
Architects' Journal, August 11, 1994.
Building Design, January 28, 1994.
Building, January 1994.
RIBA Journal, February 1996.
The Planning and Architecture Guide 1997, co-authorship prepared on behalf of The Guinness Trust.

Odedina & Allardyce, Architects

73 Leconfield Road,
London N5 2RZ
T: 0171 704 9371
F: 0171 704 9774
E: odedina@btinternet.com

Resources
2 partners, 2 assistants.
CAD facilities.

P

Professional indemnity
Yes.

Selected projects
Diamond Arts Centre, Longford School, Feltham. Adaptable performance space/studio in existing building, lottery funded, under construction 1997.
London College of Fashion. New darkrooms for photography department, £300,000, 1996.
Cochrane Theatre, London. Adaptation of existing buildings for Talawa Theatre Company/ The London Institute, £500,000, 1992.

Awards/competitions
RIAS Rowand Anderson Silver Medal.
John Keppie Scholarship.

Further reading
Architecture Today, March 1997.
Le Moniteur Architecture, June 1993
London: A guide to recent architecture.
Samantha Hardingham (Artemis) 1993
Designers Journal, September1992
The Times, September 2, 1992.
Architects' Journal September16, 1992

Page & Park Architects
Italian Centre
49 Cochrane Street
Glasgow G1 1HL
T: 0141 552 0686
F: 0141 552 1466

Resources
4 partners, 2 associates, 9 architectural staff, 2 technical staff.
CAD facilities.

Largest project value to date
£9 million.

Professional indemnity
Yes.

Selected projects
University of Strathclyde, Rottenrow Residence, Glasgow, new 146-bed student housing, £2.5 million, 1997.
Glasgow 1999, The Lighthouse Architecture and Design Centre and design-orientated retail, £9 million, due for completion 1999.
Museum of Country Life, Kittochside, new build museum for national agricultural collection, £4.5 million (£3.8m Heritage lottery funding), due for completion1999.
Holmwood House, Glasgow, repair and adaptation, in progress 19981.
Centre for Contemporary Arts, Glasgow, alteration, upgrading and extension of facilities, £5 million, 1998.

Awards/competitions
Glasgow Institute of Architecture Awards 1991, Italian Centre, Glasgow, highly commended.
Civic Trust Award 1991, Italian Centre, Glasgow.
Europa Nostra 1991, Diploma of Merit, Italian Centre, Glasgow.
Mansell Refurbishment Design Award 1991 Italian Centre, Glasgow, special commendation
Scottish Enterprise/RIAS Regeneration Design Award 1992, Supreme Award, Italian Centre, Glasgow.
Scottish Civic Trust 1992 Glasgow Award Scheme, Italian Centre, Glasgow.
British Urban Regeneration Association Best Practice Award 1995, Italian Centre, Glasgow.
Glasgow Institute of Archiecture Design Award 1993, Brodlek Visitor Reception Centre, Brodliek Castle, Isle of Arran.
Scottish Civic Trust 1992 Glasgow Award Scheme, Diploma of Excellence, St Mungo Museum, Glasgow.

Panther Hudspith Architects
235 Southwark Bridge Road
London SE1 6NP
T: 0171 407 2786
F: 0171 403 4176

Resources
2 partners, 6 architects, 6 architectural assistants, 1 office manager.

CAD Apple Macintosh facilities.

Largest project to date
10 million.

Professional indemnity
Yes.

Selected projects
Restaurant and bar, Newcastle Quayside development, £750,000, 1997.
Refurbishment of grade II listed cinema in Brighton, £350,000, 1997.
Millennium markers and visitors' centres
Ten visitors' centres between Kew Bridge and Hampton Court, £5 million, 1996.
Southwark Bridge pedestrian underpass refurbishment, London, £100,000, 1996.
New science and technology block for Hillview Secondary School, Kent, £500,000, 1996.
St Christopher's Hospice refurbishment, Lewisham, London, £120,000, 1996.
New build private house in Surrey, £400,000, 1994.
Warehouse refurbishment into new headquarters, London, £250,000, 1993.
Thames Riverside improvement proposals for the Royal Fine Arts Commission, London, 1992.

Awards/competitions
Millennium Markers and Visitor Centres Competition, 1996, winner.
Mac for the Millennium, competition for Midlands Art Centre, shortlisted.
Designers' Journal Award, 1990, second place, Studio Way, Boreham.
RIBA Regional Award,1990, second place, house, Surrey:
RIBA Regional Award (commendation), 1994.

Further Reading
Designers Journal, January 1990.
Estates Gazette, May 1989.

Parr Shearer
42 Miller Street
Glasgow G1 1DT
T/F: 0141 221 0100

Resources
2-3 staff including directors, each with own computer.
Autocad Release 13, Microsoft Office, Quicken.

Largest project to date
£5 million.

Professional Indemnity
To cover specific projects.

Selected projects
Parr Shearer home, 3 Park Terrace, Glasgow, £150,000, 1995.
Mackintosh Exhibition, Glasgow Museums, 1995.
Festival Offices for Glasgow 1999, £25,000,

1996.
Christie's Auction House, 164-166 Bath
Street, Glasgow, £250,000, on site 1997.

Awards
Sam Maver Travel Scholarship, Mackintosh
School of Architecture, 1990.
1995 Glasgow Institute of Architects Sponsors
Award.

Further reading
RIBA Journal Interiors, December 1997.
Self Build Magazine, December 1997.
Design Week, August 8, 1997.
Building Design Interiors, Summer 1997.
The Financial Times, June 4, 1996.

Patel Taylor
85 Royal College Street
London NW1 0SE
T: 0171 388 3223
F: 0171 388 3257

Resources
2 partners, 4 architects,1 landscape architect,
2 assistant architects, 1 admin.
4 CAD stations, 2 DTP terminals, laser printer,
A1 plotter.

Largest project value to date
£8 million.

Professional indemnity
Arranged project by project.

Selected projects
Music Study Centre, Hitchin, £750,000
(National lottery funded), 1997.
Aberystwth University, Cardiff, £2 million, (part
National lottery funded), 1997.
Sandringham School, St Albans, £2 million,
(National lottery funded), 1997
Seafront enhancements, Minehead,£2.75m,
(ERDF), 1997.
Southwark Embankment regeneration bid, The
Architecture Foundation's Future Southwark
design initiative, London, £1.7m, 1997.
Royal Victoria Square, £2.5m, (Government
office), 1997.
Thames Barrier, £8m, (Government office),
1997.
Thames Barrier Park, £350,000 (Government
office), 1996.
Ayr Citadel, Scotland, £1.5m (Enterprise
Authority), 1995.

Awards/competitions
Thames Barrier Park, international competition,
1995, first prize.
Hampro Hospital, national competition,1994,
second prize.
Europan 3, 1994, Pierre-Bénite, France,
first prize
Europan 3, 1994, Dordrecht, Netherlands,
first prize.
University of Amiens, invited competition,
1993, finalist.
Ayr Citadel, national competition, 1993,

first prize.
Europan 2, 1991, Châteauroux, France,
first prize.
Saltire Geddes Planning Award, 1995,
Ayr Citadel.
Glass and Glazing Award, 1995, PACE centre
Geoffrey Gribble Conservation Award,
1995, PACE centre.
Architecture Award RIBA, 1992,
Arts Centre, Wales.

Exhibitions
Royal Academy Summer Exhibition 1997.
Greenwich Millennium Pavilions, The RIBA
Journal, The Architecture Foundation, 1996.
Future Southwark, The Architecture
Foundation,1996.
Royal Academy Summer Exhibition 1996.
Milan Triennale, 1996, Thames Barrier Park.
Thames Barrier Park, The Architecture
Foundation, 1996.
Loft 2,1995, RIBA, London.
The Royals – A Bridge to the Future, RIBA,
London,1995.
New British Architecture, The Architecture
Foundation, 1994.

Further reading
Architectural Review, November 1996.
Architecture & Detail, August 1996.
RIBA Journal, May 1996.
RIBA Journal August 1996.
Architectural Review, June 1995.
RIBA Journal, April 1995.

Pawson Williams Architects
19a Floral street
Covent Garden
London WC2E 9DS
T: 0171 240 5151
F: 0171 379 8394

Resources
2 partners, 5 architects, 2 architectural staff,
1 admin.
8 networked Apple Macintosh workstations.
MiniCAD, Stratavison 3D.

Largest project value to date
£7.5 million, current projects over £15 million.

Professional indemnity
Yes.

Selected projects
Birmingham Repertory Theatre, (lottery
related) in progress 1997.
Bressingham Steam Museum, Norfolk,
feasibility study, (lottery related) in progress
1997.
Cheltenham Art Gallery, Museum & Library,
(lottery related) in progress 1997.
Farnborough Air Sciences Trust, feasibility
study, in progress 1997.
The Orange Tree theatre, Richmond, (lottery
related) in progress 1997.
The Rising Sun Arts Centre, Reading, (lottery
related) in progress 1997.

The Earth Galleries, Natural History Museum,
London, £12 million (£6 million lottery funding:
first major UK lottery assisted project)1996.

Awards/competitions
MERCAT Centre, Dingwall, invited competition
1997, winner.
Orange Tree Theatre, invited competition 1997,
winner.
North of England Concert Hall, invited
competition 1997, finalist.
Hamilton Arts Centre, limited competition
1997, 2nd place.
Cardiff Bay Opera House, open international
competition1994, selected project.
National Museum of Scotland, open RIAS
competition 1991, shortlisted.
Dulwich Gallery open RIBA competition, 1990,
shortlisted.
Cardiff Castle Visitors' Centre, open RIBA
competition, third prizewinner.

Exhibitions
Royal Academy Summer Exhibition, 1991-7.
Architecture Tomorrow, 1996.
Tokyo International Forum Exhibition, London
1990.
Walking on Glass. solo exhibition, London and
Edinburgh 1990.

Further reading
Architects' Journal, October 30,1997.
Architectural Design, August 1997.
Museum International, 196, 1997.
Architects' Journal, July 25 1996.
AJ Interiors Review, December 1996.
FX Magazine, October 1995.

Perkins Ogden Architects
Construct House
Winchester Road
Alresford
Hampshire SO24 9EZ
T: 01962 735 155
F: 01962 734 305

Resources
6 architects and 3 support staff.
Networked Apple Macintosh computers,
MiniCAD, model-making facilities.

Largest project value to date
£11.5 million.

Professional indemnity
Yes.

Selected projects
University of Portsmouth student residences,
£3,000,000, 1993.
Hackney Community College, masterplan
redevelopment, phase 1 £18.5 million, 1997;
phase 2, sports & performing arts centre
£8 million and phase 3, art & design and
media centre. £3.5 million, in progress 1997.
Sparsholt College of Agriculture, new library
and information centre, £470,000, 1996.
Greene King, new distribution depot, Yateley,

Hampshire, £900,000, 1996.

Awards/competitions
RIBA Award, 1996, Sparsholt College of
Agriculture.
RIBA Award, 1996, Greene King new
distribution depot.
RIBA Southern Region Chairman's Award,
1996, Sparsholt College of Agriculture.

Further reading
Building September 6, 1996.
Building Design, September 27, 1996.
RIBA Journal, October 1996.
The Sunday Times, February 9, 1997.
Perspectives in Architecture, April 1997.

Peter Barber Architects
11 Great Sutton Street
London EC1V 0BX
T/F: 0171 689 3555

Resources
Total staff 3 including principal.
CAD facilities.

Largest project to date
£1 million.

Professional indemnity
Yes.

Selected projects
Andrews Wharf Studios, London, £150,000,
1992.
Villa Anbar, Saudi Arabia, £200,000, 1993.
The Tower House, Clerkenwell, £150,000,
1996.
Broadway Market masterplan, London,
£1 million, 1997.
Thames Valley University, London,
£5 million, 1997.

Awards/competitions
Kordijk Biennale, Design for Europe, 1989.
Raftopolous competition, first prize, 1991.
Aga Khan Award, shortlisted, 1995.

Exhibitions
Castel San Angelo, Rome, 1995.
Desiring Practices, RIBA, London, 1995.
Hidden Art of Hackney, 1996.
Barthouse, 1997.

Further reading
Blueprint Magazine, March 1995.
QA Magazine, July 1996
Art and Design, November 1996.
Artifice Magazine, November 1996

Procter:Rihl
190c Royal College Street
London NW1 9NN
T: 0171 284 0248
F: 0171 916 1517
E: cprocter@dircon.co.uk

Resources
2 partners, 3 staff.
2 CAD workstations.

Largest project value to date
£500,000.

Professional indemnity
Yes.

Selected projects
Apartment building, Brazil, £500,000, in progress 1997.
Space Lily Garden for Commes des Garçons Shop, Tokyo, in progress, 1997.
Topo Furniture, range of shelving, London, 1997.
Loft conversion for a film producer, Shoreditch, London,1997.
Soho penthouse, extension and reworking of duplex, London, £64,000, 1996.
Mansion Block, flat conversion, Battersea, London, £70,000, in progress 1997.

Awards/competitions
International Design Yearbook, nominated May 1998.
Blueprint Design Awards, 1997, 3rd prize.
Architecture Fellowship, Arts Foundation, nominated 1996.
Variazioni, Modo Magazine/Cascina, Italy, finalist 1996.

Furthor roading
RIBA Journal, September 1997.
Harper's Bazaaar, USA, September 1997.
Blueprint, September1997.
Blueprint, November 1997.
Elle Decoration, September 1997.
Modo, Italy, March 1997.
Wallpaper, January 1997.

Richard Murphy Architects
34 Blair Street
Edinburgh EH1 1QR
T: 0131 220 6125
F: 0131 220 6781

Resources
1 principal architect, 4 architects,
5 architectural assistants (RIBA Part II),
2 architectural assistants (RIBA Part I),
1 CAD technician and 1 admin.
3 CAD workstations, A1 design jet printer, colour scanner, Zip drive. NBS full disc service and Darbour microfilm technical index.

Largest project value to date
£5.8 million.

Professional indemnity
Yes.

Selected projects
Renovation, Fruitmarket Gallery, Edinburgh, 1993, £330,000.
17 Royal Terrace Mews conversion, Edinburgh, 1995, £100,000.
Cancer Care Centre, Western General Hospital, Edinburgh, 1996, £127,000.
Office conversion, including fit out for Royal Fine Art Commission, Edinburgh,1997, £200,000.
Dundee City Arts Centre, on site 1997, £5.8 million.
Harmeny residential school, Balerno, on site, £2 million.

Awards/competitions
RIBA Award 1993, Fruitmarket Gallery, Edinburgh.
RIBA Award 1995, 49 Gilmour Road, Edinburgh.
Royal Scottish Academy Gold Medal for Architecture 1995, experimental energy house.
RIBA Award 1996, 17 Royal Terrace Mews, Edinburgh.
EAA Silver Medal 1996, 7 Abbotsford Park, Edinburgh.
EAA Conservation Award 1996 and RIBA Award 1997, Cancer Caring Centre, Edinburgh
Stirling prize, shortlisted 1996 and 1997.

Further reading
The Herald, May 26, 1997.
Architects' Journal, March 13, 1997.
The Scotsman, October 15, 1996.
Scotland on Sunday, July 14, 1996.
Architects' Journal, September 21, 1995.

Russell Light Architectural Design
68 Gell Street
Sheffield S3 7QW
T: 0114 275 7214
F: 0114 270 6607
E: R.D.Light@sheffield.ac.uk

Resources
2 partners/architects.
Macintosh systems, MiniCAD and Microstation.

Largest project value to date
£200,000.

Professional indemnity
Project by project basis.

Selected projects
House extension, Totley, Sheffield, 1997.
Barn conversion, Stoney Middleton, 1997.
Mitchell Field Farm, connecting link, Hathersage, £10,000, 1994.
Mitchell Field Farm, barn conversion, 1994.
The Orchard, Calver, Derbyshire, £200,000, 1991.

Further reading
Building Design, October 20, 1996.
Design Week, August 29, 1996.
Building Design, Jan 27, 1995.
Building Design, July 28, 1996.
Perspectives, March 1995.
Architectural Research Quarterly, Winter 1995.

Sarah Wigglesworth
10 Stock Orchard Street
London N7 9RW
T: 0171 607 9200
F: 0171 607 5800

Resources
1 director, 2 architects.
3 Apple Macintosh computers.

Largest project value to date
£1.6 million.

Professional indemnity
Yes.

Selected projects
House in Chelsea, London, remodelling,
£50,000, 1995.
Strawbale House, north London, novel
materials, straw bale walls, £400,000, on site
1998.
Studios for Siobhan Davies Dance Company,
£1.6 million lottery bid, December 1997.
Writer's retreat, all-wood garden pavilion
prototype, £20,000, in progress,1997.

Awards/competitions
Europan competition 1993, honorary mention.
Burgess Park Gateways, Southwark,
London,1993, runner up.

Exhibitions
Drawing on Diversity, 1997.
RIBA Heinz Gallery, London June/July 1997.
Desiring Practices, exhibitions designed and
project managed at sites all over London,
1995.

Further reading
Perspectives, June/July 1997.
Architectural Review, June/July 1997.
Architects' Journal, July 1997.
Perspectives, Oct/Nov 1997.
RIBA Journal, November 1997.
Drawing on Diversity catalogue, 1997.

Sauerbruch Hutton architects
74 Ledbury Road
London W11 2AH
T: 0171 221 0105
F: 0171 792 9894
E: sharc@compuserve.com

Lehrter Strasse 57
10557 Berlin
T: 49 30 397 821 0
F: 49 30 397 821 00

Resources
London office: 2 architects, 2 technical staff.
Berlin office: 6 architects, 6 architectural staff,
2 technical staff and 2 admin. Computer
network between offices.

Largest project value to date
£65 million.

Professional indemnity
Yes.

Selected projects
GSW Headquarters in Berlin, now under
construction, completion early 1999,
£60 million.
Conversion of 1960s villa with an indoor
swimming pool, London, 1995, £190,000.
Conversion of Victorian house, London, 1995,
£190,000.
Refurbishment of Benenden School, 1997.
Centre for innovation in Photonics, Berlin,
under construction 1997, £22 million.

Awards/competitions
Olympic cycling and swimming hall for Berlin
and Alsenblock, competition entry,1992.
Offices for the German President, competition
entry, 1994.
Government offices ' Alsenblock ', Berlin, fourth
prize, 1994.
Urban Masterplan, Schwerin, second prize, 1997.

Further reading
London: World Cities, Academy Editions,
London 1994.
Houses for Sale, exhibition catalogue, Cologne,
1996.
Frontiers. Artists and Architects. Academy
Group, London, 1997.
Architecture in the New Landscape, Projects
1990 – 1996, Birkhauser Verlag, Basel.

Saville Jones Architects
3 Teville Place, Worthing
West Sussex BN11 1UQ
T: 01903 211363
F: 01903 211114

Resources
2 partners, 1 assistant architect, 1 technician.
2 Apple Macintosh workstations, MiniCAD,
Photoshop and Illustrator. 1PC, Caddie (CAD)
and Heatloss programme.

Largest project value to date
£4.2 million, feasibility study for project of
£15 million.

Professional indemnity
Yes.

Selected projects
Newbury District Council, swimming pool,
Berkshire, 1997, £1.2 million.
Swimming Pool, Les Quennevais, Jersey, 1996,
£4.2 million.
Mountain Leisure Centre, refurbishment, 1996,
£600,000.
Private indoor pool, Hove, 1997, £105,000.
Broadwater Baptist Church, Worthing,
extension, 1996, £200,000.

Awards/competitions
Royal Borough of Windsor & Maidenhead
Architectural & Environmental Award Scheme
1994, Magnet Leisure Centre, Maidenhead.

Sergison Bates Architects
44 Newman Street
London W1P 3PA
T: 0171 255 1564
F: 0171 636 5646

Resources
2 architects, 2 architectural assistants,
1 part-time admin.
Power Macintosh network, 3 workstations:
MiniCAD.

Largest project value to date
£520,000. Feasibility studies up to £3 million.

Professional indemnity
Yes.

Selected projects
Public House, Walsall, £520,000, 1997
(with Caruso St John Architects).
Towards 2001 exhibition design, Royal Festival
Hall, London, 1997.
Jaeger House refurbishment, Soho,
London, 1997.
Private residence, Belgravia, London,
£125,000, 1996.
Montessori Nursery School, London,
£70,000, 1996.

Exhibitions
Under 50K, RIBA October 1992.
Public Views, The Architecture Foundation,
1995.
Europan IV, Royal Festival Hall, February 1997.
Sittingbourne Settlement Competition, RIBA,
July 1997.
Smithfield Market Exhibition, Dublin, August
1997.

Further reading
Le Moniteur Architecture, Paris, Feb 1995.
Architects' Journal, July 13, 1995.
Europan Competition Winners Catalogue,
March 1997.
RIBA Journal, October 1997.
Blueprint, November 1997.

Shed KM
TheTea Factory
92 Wood Street
Liverpool L1 4DQ
T: 0151 709 8211
F: 0151 708 8266
E: arch2shed.u-net.com

Resources
3 partners, 10 staff.
Fully equipped Apple Mac based studio.

Largest project value to date
£10 million.

Professional indemnity
Yes.

Selected projects
Architecture Studio. Liverpool University

£1,000,000, 1988.
Student Services, Liverpool University
£1,700,000, 1994.
Concert Square buildings, Urban Splash,
£2,500,000, 1995,
Schoolhouse and annexe, Urban Splash,
£1,400,000,1996.
Rococomodo, Baa Bar, £900,000,1997.
Match Factory Phase I,1997.

Awards
RIBA Award1996,Concert Square.
RIBA Award1996, Schoolhouse.
RIBA Award1997, Rococomodo.
British Urban Regeneration Award for Best
Practice, Concert Square.
Concert Square, Merseyside Civic Society
Award for Conservation.

Snell Associates
50b Abbey Gardens
St. John's Wood
London NW8 9AT
T: 0171 328 6593
F: 0171 372 6771

Resources
1 partner, 3 architects, 2 architectural staff,
1 admin.
4 Apple Macintosh CAD
workstations,Microstation, desktop publishing
and 3D Photoshop.

Largest project value to date
£4 million.

Professional indemnity
Yes.

Selected projects
Ryde Pier visitor centre and masterplan,
Isle of Wight, £6 million, in progress1997.
Rooftop penthouse, Frobisher House,
Chelsea, £250,000, 1997.
Pavilion Theatre Canopy, Worthing Pier,
£200,000, in progress 1997.
Northern Architecture Centre, Newcastle,
£4 million, (lottery funded) in progress, 1997.
Foyer art galley, Surrey Institute of Art &
Design, Farnham, £500,000, (lottery funded)
in progress 1997.
Extension to Michael Hopkins' Offices, London,
£150,000, 1995.
L8 Summer House, Finland. £1.5million, in
progress 1997.

Awards/competitions
First prize, Northern Architecture Centre 1995,
RIBA competition.
First prize, Worthing Canopy Competition
1996.
First prize, Surrey Institute of Art and Design.

Exhibitions
Picking Winners, exhibition of National Lottery
projects, RIBA 1997.

Further reading
Architects' Journal, March 28, 1996
Architects' Journal, July 4, 1996
Architects' Journal, October 31, 1996.
Architects' Journal, April 20, 1995.
Detail, December 1995.

Spencer Fung Architects
No. 3 Pine Mews
London NW10 3JA
T: 0181 960 9339
F: 0181 960 9883

Resources
1 partner, 1 architect,
Apple Mac CAD system, graphic and model
making skills.

Largest project value to date
£2 million.

Professional indemnity
Yes.

Selected projects
Apartment Building, Japan,1990.
Designers Guild, North Kensington, London,
£350,000,1992.
Isometrix Office, Clerkenwell, London,1993.
Hotel La Gazelle d'Or, Taroundant,
Morocco,1994.
Shopping Centre, Ait Mellou, Morocco, 1994.
Own Apartment, Belsize Park, London, 1996.
Home Furniture range, 1997.
1997 Office Building, Barbican, London,1997.

Stan Bolt: Architect
The Old Musuem
Higher Street
Brixham
Devon TQ5 8HW
T: 01803 852 588

Resources
Sole practitioner, 2 technicians as needed.

Largest project value to date
£250,000.

Professional indemnity
Yes.

Selected projects
Clann House Residential Home, Lanivet,
extension, £50,000, 1997.
Office extension, Zeneca Ltd, £100,000,
1995.
The New School, Exminster, additional
accommodation, £36,500, 1997.
Annex to 7 Plymouth Road, Totnes, £12,000,
1994.
Sleeman House, Lanjeth, residential home,
£100,000, 1994.

Awards/competitions
RIBA Regional Award 1997, New School
Exminster.
RIBA Regional Award 1995, Plymouth Road.
RIBA Regional Award 1993, shortlisted.

Stephen Donald Architects Ltd.
45 Mitchell Street
London EC1V 3QD
T: 0171 490 0665
F: 0171 490 1455
E:@aphasia.demon.co.uk

Resources
5 full-time staff.
PowerMacs with MiniCAD.

Largest project value to date
£2 million.

Professional indemnity
Yes.

Selected projects
The Office Bar and Nightclub, Rathbone Place,
£100,000, 1997.
Café/Bar in former NatWest Bank site,
Centre Point, London, £550,000,
due to complete April 1998.
Gamelan Performance Arts Centre,
Royal Schools for the Deaf, Manchester,
£2 million (Lottery bid), 1997.
Jazz Venue, Blvd. de Clichy, Paris, £2million,
1997.
Cube Bar, London NW3, £650,000, 1996.

Further reading
Archi Creé, September 1997.
AD Monograph, March 1996.
Architecture Today, October 1996.

Studio 8 Architects
95 Greencroft Gardens
London NW6 3PG
T: 0171 624 5768
F: 0171 625 8520

Resources
5 full time staff.
A computer collaborator works on specific
projects.

Largest project to date
£70,000. Pending £10 million project.

Professional indemnity
No.

Selected projects
LASH Roller Hockey Centre, Stratford, London,
£4 million, 1997.
SW Sushi Bar, Kensington, London, fit out,
£70,000, 1997.
Cultural Centre at University College London,
won international competition, £10 million,
1996.

Awards/competitions
Bridge of the Future, Japan, 2nd prize, 1987.
Housing a Demonstration Project,1st Prize,
1988.
SXL Residential Design Competition, Japan,
Honourable Mention.
AA in Asia – The Next Generation, group
exhibition travelling around Asia Pacific, 1996.
Public Views 2: Architecture, Film, Theory,
Music, Art and Things, group exhibition, The
Architecture Foundation, 1997.

Further reading
Domus, October 1997.
441/10....We'll Reconfigure the Space When
You're Ready" IND E8 London 1996.
"Light Registers from London" Form Zero, USA
1998.

Studio BAAD
Linden Mill
Linden Road
Hebden Bridge
West Yorkshire HX7 7DN
T: 01422 843045
F: 01422845464
E:L baad.demon.co.uk.

Resources
Total Staff, 15, 12 architects or assistant
architects
CAD facilities.

Largest project to date
£5.2 million

Professional indemnity
Yes.

Selected projects
Simon Jersey 2, garment company HQ and
distribution building, Accrington,1991.
Accident and Emergency Department,
Fazakerley Hospital,1991-93.
Office, showroom & distribution building,
Manchester,1993.
Refurbishment of Grade II listed church for
offices, 1993.
Refurbishment of 10,000 sq m. mill for mixed
use, 1993.
New entrance and glass canopy, Teesside,
1995.
Conversation of existing mill to art gallery, West
Yorkshire, 1995.
Refurbishment of timber framed barn,
Berkshire, 1996.

Awards/competitions
Design & Build submission for Accident &
Emergency Department, Fazakerley Hospital,
Liverpool, winning design,1991.
International Design competition, New
University of Cyprus, shortlisted, 1993.
Art Gallery café/restaurant, Hull, second place,
1991.

Exhibitions

New British Architecture, The Architecture Foundation, 1994.
Emerging British Architecture.
AJ Centenary Exhibition, Business Design Centre, London,1995.
Eminent & Imminent, Site Gallery, Leeds, 1997.

Further reading

Architecture Today, February 1992.
AJ Focus, October 1992.
Architects' Journal, 28 April 1993.
Architects' Journal, 6 July 1994.
Architects' Journal, 19 October 1995.

Studio Downie Architects

146 New Cavendish Street
London W1M 7FG
T: 0171 255 1599
F: 0171 636 7883

Resources

Staff 6: Craig Downie, principal, 2 senior architects, assistants from Part I to III.
Computer MAC systems / MiniCAD.

Largest project value to date

£5 million

Professional indemnity

Yes.

Selected projects

French Treasury, new office, etc., Piccadilly, London, £250,000, 1994.
Opportunity and Community Arts Centre, Southall, £1 million, 1996.
BAA-Lynton, commercial office building, London, re-imaging/refurbishment, £1 million, 1998 completion.
Corpus Christi College, Cambridge, feasibility study, new museum, rare book facility and conservation centre within a Grade I listed building.
Hat Hill Sculpture Foundation, The Goodwood Estate, 20 acre outdoor sculpture display and landscaping with a new gallery, £250,000, 1995.
DTI/DfEE European Funded IT Information Centres, West London, £1.25 million, ongoing.

Awards/competitions

National Winner of Design Business Award, 1995.
Shortlisted Project for Building Construction Industry Awards, Hat Hill Sculpture Gallery, 1995.
Commendation EMAP Architecture Tomorrow Awards, Hat Hill Sculpture Gallery, 1995.

Exhibitions

'Emerging UK Architects', 1994, RIBA exhibition and seminar series, Architectural Institute of Japan.
Solo Exhibition, August 1996, RIBA, Hat Hill Sculpture Foundation and Gallery.

Further reading

Architectural Review, Nov 1997.
Sequence Bois, 5 Sept 1996.
Architecture Cree, Aug/Sept 1996.
RIBA Journal, May 1996.
Architects' Journal, 25 April 1996.
Architects' Journal, 28 Sept 1995.
Architectural Review, Aug 1996.
World Architecture, No.34.

Studio MG Architects

4th Floor
101 Turnmill Street
London EC1M 5QP
T: 0171 251 2648
F: 0171 490 8070

Resources

2 partners, 2 associates and up to 6 staff as necessary.
3-6 Macintosh workstations, as project requires, MiniCAD.

Largest project value to date

£1.6 million.

Professional indemnity

Yes

Selected projects

Dental Surgery, Islington, semi-new build, £100,000, 1997.
6 semi-new build houses in 1920s building, Putney, London,1997.
Conversion of Listed school building into 25 apartments, Putney, London, £800,000, 1996.
Loft apartment with blue glass walls, Clerkenwell, London, £5,000, 1996.
Penthouses, The Barbican, London, £45,000, 1995.

Awards/competitions

Financial Times Millennium Footbridge, St Paul's, London,1996, exhibited.
Butagas Housing, Montreuil Maric, 1996, 2nd prize.
Newcastle Architecture Centre, 1995, exhibited.
Yokohama Ferry Terminal, Japan, 1995, exhibited.

Exhibitions

Co-Curators, 'Living Design', RIBA and touring, 1997.
Curators, 'The Big Shelf', proposed for Imagination Gallery, Spring1998.

Further reading

FX, Sept/Oct 1997.
Architects' Journal, 5 Sept 1997.
Building Design, 22 August 1997.
RIBA Journal, August 1997.
World Architecture, no. 40 July 1996.
Perspectives, December 1995.

T

The Architects Practice

23 Beacon Hill
London N7 9LY
T: 0171 607 3333
F: 0171 700 7066
E: ArchPractice@compuserve.com
W: architects-practice.com

Resources

1 permanent member of staff, Simon Foxell.
2 Apple Macintosh workstations with internet access.

Largest project to date

£1.4 million

Professional indemnity

Yes.

Selected projects

Dover Castle, Keepyard Shop for English Heritage, £80,000, 1989.
Jeff Banks in-store design for House of Fraser, value dependent on installation, 1991.
House refurbishment, Exercise Pavilion, Highgate, London, 1995.
Office refurbishment, South Bank, London, £50,000,1997.

Awards/competitions

DuPont Benedictus Award, winner, 1996.
British Construction Industry Awards, finalist, 1996.
Glassex Industry Awards, Building of the Year, runner-up, 1996.

Further reading

Bibliotecha Alexandrina, Exhibition Catalogue, Unesco 1990.
Which, September 1994.
Architects' Journal, 6 June 1996.
Building Design, July 1996.
L'Area, September1996.
Techniques & Architecture, October-November 1996.
Architectural Design, Profile No.126, 1997.

Thomas Croft Architect

17 Hatton Street
London NW8 8PL
T: 0171 724 7270
F: 0171 724 6018
E: tomcroft@aol.com

Resources

1 principal and 1 assistant (due to expand Spring 1998).
Apple Macintosh Power PC computers.

Largest project value to date

£600,000

Professional indemnity

Yes

Selected projects

Royal Yacht Squadron Pavilion, Isle of Wight, new-build entertainment building, on site

1998.
Junior King's School, Canterbury, renovation of tithe barn, feasibility study, 1997.
Timothy Taylor Gallery, Bruton Place, London W1, 1996.
Shepherdess Walk, London N1, masterplanning loft development, 1995-6.
Rayham Barn, Whitstable, renovation of Grade II barn, 1988.

Awards/competitions
AJ/Bovis Royal Academy Summer Exhibition prize, 1988.

Further reading
Perspectives, October 1997.
RIBA Journal, March 1997.
Perspectives, May 1996.
Vogue, November 1995.

Vaughan & McIlhenny Architects
The Town House
17 Cathedral Square
Fortrose, Ross & Cromarty
Aberdeen IV10 8TB
T: 01381 621373

Resources
2 partners, 1 final year- out student.
Work produced on drawing boards, but all staff trained in CAD.

Largest project to date
£2.5 million

Professional indemnity
Yes.

Selected projects
Boathouse, Ardarroch, House and garage, Value £93,462.
Church Street, Cromarty, renovation of Grade C listed building, £70,000.
Knockmuir Lodge, Fortrose, house extension, £40,000.
Old Bakery, Fortrose, renovation of bakery and stables to form 2 houses, £100,000.
Playgroup, Fortrose, new build, £100,000.
Wick, renovation of 19th century fishery town at Lower Pulteney, £2.5 million.

Further reading
"Gordon Cullen Visions of Urban Design" by David Gosling, Academy Editions, 1996.

Walter Menteth + Graham Little Architects
1a Iliffe Street, Kennington
London SE17 3QA
T: 0171 708 5825
F: 0171 252 4742

Walter Menteth and Graham Little no longer practice together. Walter Mentheth Architects practices from the above address. Graham Little practices as :

Plat.form
48d Clerkenwell Close
London EC1R 0AJ
T/F: 0171 490 0918

Selected projects
2-4 Gwynne Road, Battersea, London, 8 self-contained flats, 1997.
Private residences, Dominica and Jamaica, 1997.
69 Bloomfield Road, Woolwich, London, residential group home, 1997.
7 Tyers Gate, London, private mixed development, 1997.

Awards/competitions
Concrete Society Award, shortlisted, 1994.

Exhibitions
Edinburgh Haymarket Competition, The Royal High Exhibition, October 1995.
First Sight Exhibition, (3 projects), RIBA Gallery, London, April-May 1995.
Before + After Design + Build Exhibition, RIBA Gallery, London, Jan-Feb 1994.

Further reading
RIBA Journal Interiors, Dec 1996.
Europa Forum Wien, November 1996.
Homes & Ideas, April 1996.

Walters and Cohen
Second Floor, Block E
Carkers Lane, 53 79 Highgate Road
London NW5 1TL
T: 0171 428 9751
F: 0171 428 9752
E: @walco.netkonect.co.uk

Resources
2 partners, 1 architect, 4 other architectural staff.
8 workstations, central server, 3D modelling.

Largest project value to date
£3 million.

Professional indemnity
Yes.

Selected projects
New art gallery and workshops, Durban, South Africa, 1.5million South African Rands, 1996.
Four penthouses in Chelsea, London, £2.2 million.
Jigsaw Day Nursery, Bristol, £550,000.

Holmes Place Health Club, Chelsea, London, £500,000.
Queens House offices, London, £600,000.
Tobago Beach House, West Indies, 1 million Trinidad and Tobago dollars.

Awards/competitions
Recently shortlisted for RIBA competition to design a Memorial Chapel to the Falklands War.
New Law Faculty Building, University of Cambridge, first prize.

Further reading
RIBA Journal, June 1997
Architectural Review, January 1997
World Architecture, October 1996

Wells MacKereth Architects
Unit 14 Archer Street Studios
10-11 Archer Street
London W1V 7HG
T: 0171 287 5504
F: 0171 287 5506
E: wellsmackereth@btinternet.com

Resources
Total Staff: 6
CAD facilities.

Largest project value to date
£750,000.

Professional indemnity
Yes.

Selected projects
Soho Apartment, London, 1995.
Polygon Bar and Grill, London, 1996.
Bunty Matthia's Contemporary Dance Set, London, 1996.
Apartment for a Cardiologist, London, 1997.

Further reading
The Sunday Times, 8 October 1995.
Blueprint Magazine, October 1995.
Interni Magazine (Italy) July 1996.
Blueprint Magazine, Jan 1997.
Time Out, 13-20 November 1996.
Tatler, January 1997.
Eat Soup, December 1996.
ES Magazine, 1 November 1996.
London Evening Standard, 19 November 1996.
The Guardian, 9 December 1996.
Blueprint Magazine, December 1996.
The Times, 13 December 1997.

Woolf Architects
39 – 51 Highgate Road
London NW5 1RT
Tel: 0171 428 0500
F: 0171 428 9555
E: woolfj@aol.com

Resources
2 architects, 2 architectural assitants

3 Apple Macintosh workstations (1 Power Mac), 1 Apple Macintosh admin workstations

Largest project value to date
£650,000.

Professional indemnity
Yes.

Selected projects
Lim House, London, £185,000, 1997.
Ziggurat Studios, London, £110,000, 1997.
Fellner House, London, £275,000, 1995.
Design Bridge Studios, Clerkenwell Close, London, £100,000, 1994
Ijaz apartment, London, £45,000, 1991.

Awards/competitions
Urban regeneration Smithfield, Dublin, international competition, 1991, in collaboration with Jonathan McDowell and Renato Benedetti, first prize.
Office for the year 2000, international ideas competition, Milan, 1991, in collaboration with H Langston-Jones, first prize.
Europan 1996-97, Manchester site, shortlisted.

Exhibitions
Papers on Architecture, July 1995, The Architecture Foundation.
30 Under 50k, November 1992, RIBA, London and UK touring exhibition.
Whose House Is It Anyway?, Spring 1995, Aram Showroom, Hampstead, London.

Further reading
Architects' Journal January 26, 1995.
Architects' Journal October 2, 1991.
RIBA Journal, November 1992.
Building Design, November 1, 1992.
Vogue Magazine, December 1996.

Zombory-Moldovan Moore
5 Bedale Street
London SE1 9AL
Tel: 0171 378 9990
Fax: 0171 378 9995

Resources
2 partners, 1 associate, 2 architects, 1
architectural assistant and 1 admin. staff.
MacOS CAD networked workstations:
MiniCAD, Photoshop & QuarkXPress;
image-scanning, colour-plotting, dtp.

Largest project value to date
£2.5 million

Professional indemnity
Yes.

Selected projects
Galleries and residence for private art
collection, Holland Park, £750,000, completion
March 1998.
Auction rooms, foyer and exhibition area for
Sotheby's, New Bond Street, £1 million, phases
1+2 complete, phase 3 Autumn 1998.
Studios and exhibition space, Islington, London,
£750,000, 1991/2.
Capsule micro-room hotel, South Bank,
London, £1.3 million, in progress, completion
end 1998.
Terraced house and swimming pool for art
collector, Notting Hill, London, £1.7 million,
completion end 1999.

Awards/competitions
New Paolozzi Galleries, Edinburgh, shortlisted.
Rising Sun Arts Centre, Reading, shortlisted.

Further reading
The Independent Magazine, 13 July 1996.
Perspectives, March 1995.
Building Design, 17 September 1993.

Zoo Architects
Top Floor
Central House
50 – 58 Jamaica Street
Glasgow G1 4QG
T: 0141 221 6757
F: 0141 221 6767
E-mail: pr @ zoo. u – net. com

Resources
Staff: 2 architects, 2 architectural assistants,
1 admin. and 1 urbanist.
3 Apple Mac Power workstations;
1 Motorola StarMAX CAD workstation;
1 PC workstation with AutoCAD;
A1 Calcomp 720 inkjet plotter;
Powerdraw, PowerCAD, 3D – Studio, Form Z,
Photoshop, Modelshop.

Largest project value to date
£3 million.

Professional indemnity
Yes.

Selected projects
187 NHS Trust, Adolescent & Child Psychiatry,
£250,000, 1995.
Tree Structure, Buchanan Street, Glasgow,
£30,000, 1995.
Triangle Community Arts Centre, Edinburgh,
£800,000, 1996.
Todd Building, Glasgow, Loft Showflat,
£30,000, 1997.
Manchester Street, Liverpool, Public Space
at Mersey Tunnel, £900,000, 1997.
Tramway, Glasgow, Arts Complex
Refurbishment, £2.5 million, 1997.

Competitions
Ronaldson's Wharf, Edinburgh, Short Listed,
Open Competition, 1994.
Tree Structure, Glasgow, 1st Prize, Open
Competition, 1995.
Manchester St, Liverpool, 1st Prize, Open
Competition, 1997.
Tramway, Glasgow, 1st Prize, Invited
Competition, 1997.

Further reading
L.A.D.T. Publication on Manchester Street
competition, 1997.
Architects' Journal, 10 July 1997.

All information collated, November 1997

Appendix 2

The Royal Institute of British Architects' Clients Advisory Service

The RIBA Clients Advisory Service (CAS) exists to assist clients in their selection of architects, initially by providing free lists of suitable practices according to the information provided by the client on their potential project. The information comes from an extensive database of all RIBA registered practices throughout the UK.

This unique service is available to anyone contemplating any building project and is designed to cater for both experienced clients and those who are building for the first time.

The information held on each practice includes:
- a practice profile
- sectors within which the practice has worked
- the range of services offered by the practice

The service operates from the RIBA headquarters in London:
Clients Advisory Service
Royal Institute of British Architects
66 Portland Place
London W1N 4AD
T: 0171 307 3700
F: 0171 436 9112

The Royal Incorporation of Architects in Scotland (RIAS) should also be contacted for information on any Scottish practices:
Royal Incorporation of Architects in Scotland
15 Rutland Square
Edinburgh
EH1 2BE
T. 0131 229 7205
F: 0131 228 2188

Regional Index

Scotland

Aberdeen

Vaughan & Mcllhenny   124

Edinburgh

Allan Murray Architects   20
E&F McLachlan Architects   45
John Brennan Architect   65
Lee Boyd Partnership   69
Malcolm Fraser Architects   71
Richard Murphy Architects   99

Glasgow

Anderson Christie Architects   21
McInnes Gardner & Partners   78
Page & Park Architects   86
Parr Shearer   90
Zoo Architects   131

England

North West

Harrison Ince   62
Hodder Associates   59
Ian Simpson Architects   64
OMI Architects   84
Shed KM   108

Yorkshire

Bareham Andrews Architects   26
Russell Light Architectural Design   100
Studio BAAD   116

Midlands

Bryant and Priest Architecture   34

East Anglia

Beevor Mull Architects   27
Ellis-Miller Architects & Designers   50

London

Adjaye and Russell   16
AEM   18
Allford Hall Monaghan Morris Architects   23
Apicella Associates   24
Bere: Architects   28
Birds Portchmouth Russum   29
Boyarsky Murphy Architects   30
Brady +Mallalieu Architects   31
Brooks Stacey Randall   32
Bushcow Henley   37
Carter Reynolds   35
Caruso St John   38
Cottrell and Vermeulen Architects   41
David Mikhail Architects   42
de Rijke Marsh Morgan   47
East   48
FAT   49
Foreign Office Architects Ltd   53
Gollifer Associates   54
Harper Mackay   55
Hawkins / Brown Architects   56

Hudson Featherstone   60
Hugh Broughton Architects   63
Knott Architects   68
Loader and Brown Architects   70
MacCreanor + Lavington   72
Mark Fisher Architects   74
Matthew Lloyd Architects   75
Matthew Preistman Architects   77
McDowell + Benedetti   81
MUF Architects   79
Niall McLaughlin Architects   82
Odedina & Allardyce   85
Panter Hudspith Architects   89
Patel Taylor   93
Pawson Williams Architects   87
Peter Barber Architects   96
Proctor: Rihl   91
Sarah Wigglesworth Architects   102
Sauerbruch Hutton Architects   105
Sergison Bates Architects   118
Snell Associates   110
Spencer Fung Architects   113
Stephen Donald Architects Ltd   114
Studio 8 Architects   115
Studio Downie Architects   119
Studio MG Architects   120
The Architects Practice   123
Thomas Croft Architect   121
Walter Menteth + Graham Little Architects   125
Walters and Cohen   127
Wells MacKereth Architects   128
Woolf Architects   129
Zombory-Moldavan Moore   130

South East

Alistair Howe Architect   17
Saville Jones Architects   106

South West

David Sheppard Architect   44
John Pardey Architect   67
Perkins Ogden Architects   95
Stan Bolt: Architect   103

Sponsor's comment

Today, British designers lead the architectural world. Names like Rogers, Foster, Wilkinson and Grimshaw have become bywords for stylish, elegant and innovative building design and have set the standards for today's young design professionals.

As we prepare for the third Millennium, the opportunities for shaping the built environment have never been greater or more important to our future. By supporting this exciting and important publication, British Steel is delighted to be championing the next generation of architects who will take the profession on to even greater heights.

British Steel

Thanks

The Architecture Foundation would like to thank the following sponsors, organisations and individuals who have generously contributed to the success of this project

British Steel

Glasgow 1999
UK City of
Architecture
and Design

Wordsearch Communications
Peter Murray
Lee Mallett
Sam Worthington

Phillip Evans
Esther Waterfield
Christine King
Kester Rattenbury

Clugston

All the architects and assessors involved

Panel One:
David Chipperfield (chair), David Chipperfield Architects
Rowan Moore, The Daily Telegraph Architectural Critic
Tony Hunt, Anthony Hunt Associates
Cathi Wheatley, BBC Television Producer
Prof Christine Hawley, The Bartlett School of Architecture, UCL

Panel Two:
Kirsty Wark (chair), Television Presenter
Sebastian Tombs, Secretary & Treasurer, The Royal Incorpration of Architects in Scotland
Bryan Jefferson, Architectural Advisor to the Department of Culture, Media & Sport
Richard Burdett, Trustee of the Architecture Foundation and Director, City Policy, Architecture & Engineering, London School of Economics